TRAINING AND SHOWING THE WESTERN TRAIL HORSE

DARLENE SORDILLO

ARCO PUBLISHING COMPANY, INC.
NEW YORK

Photos are by the author except where otherwise indicated.

Published by Arco Publishing Company, Inc.
219 Park Avenue South, New York, N.Y. 10003

Library of Congress Catalog Card Number 74-27438
ISBN 0-668-03757-1

Printed in the United States of America

To my husband Don,
who gave me the opportunity
and the encouragement
to write this book.

ACKNOWLEDGMENTS

To those who gave of their time and of themselves to assist in taking the photos for this book:

R. A. Greene, DVM, Editor-Publisher of *Horse, of Course!* magazine, and owner of Derbyshire Farm, Temple, New Hampshire.

Bob Webster, trainer, from Vermont.

Sheila Jansen, owner of Brimfull Stables, Hampton Falls, New Hampshire.

Conrad and Shirley Smith, owners of Iron Moon Farm, Newbury, Massachusetts.

Donna Stevens, instructor, Green Acres Stables, Dover, New Hampshire.

Contents

Introduction

A western trail horse can be the most exciting horse you've ever owned. Training this type of horse for performance in show and trail rides is a long, constant process, but any western rider worth his salt knows that the training pays off in the end.

Unlike English training, which depends mainly on a tractable horse with smooth gaits, a western performance horse must receive a more all-around training. While English horses are prized for gentle dispositions, the fiery spark of a trail horse also used for gymkhana events is highly valued by western riders.

Even more important than the western performance horse's disposition is his versatility: he must be trained in pleasure gaits, remain calm when handled by a judge, be able to pour on a burst of speed and then "stop on a dime," and be able to negotiate obstacles and jump. This is far more than what is asked of the English performance horse, who can only be ridden by an equitation rider.

The western trail horse used for performance lives a demanding life. He is required to do quick sprints, to endure long trail rides, and most important, to be trustworthy at all times.

A competitive western rider must always be able to count on his trail horse. When you're loping along a wooded trail during a competitive ride and a brook suddenly looms up ahead, you have to know your mount will jump it without shying away from the moving water. The rider directs his horse, but he also must be able to anticipate his horse's actions. Only a horse who is trustworthy and consistent will make a winning trail competitor.

The key to successful western showing is an expert rider teamed with a well-trained horse, both working in perfect coordination and timing with each other. The only way to achieve this is through understanding, dedication, and practice. With these three elements under your hat, you're on your way to becoming a top western trail competitor.

1. Choosing the Trail Horse

Since a trail horse must have talent in several areas, a good show prospect may be hard to come by. However, the best trail horses are not bought fully trained.

The western rider who trains his own trail horse will have a better show prospect in the end, since the horse and rider will develop their own communication and timing during the training period. The horse who takes blue ribbons in a trail class under one rider may not perform as well for you initially—it takes practice to make a winning horse-and-rider team.

Theoretically, any horse can be trained for western trail events, but certain horses are more suited to trail work than others. It is important to understand what you are looking for before you buy your trail horse prospect.

The most important feature of a trail horse is reliability. An unpredictable horse just will not do. This stands to reason when you consider the origin of trail rides and show classes.

The western cowhands who had to ride days on end through

isolated mountain trails obviously needed horses they could count on. When the first horse shows and competitive trail rides were organized, the quality most important to the old trail riders became the most highly prized element in a trail class. The western trail performance horse must, above all else, be trustworthy.

The novice may have a hard time judging this attribute in a horse, but there are telltale signs to watch for. Observe any horse you are considering buying for use in trail events from the ground up. If he is skittish, or has nasty habits like biting and kicking, you don't want him. Look the horse in the eye, just as you would when meeting a new human. A wild look in his eyes, or a constant habit of flattening his ears back and swinging his head around is an indication of a bad temper. Stay away from horses like this, for they will be of no use in trail competition.

As a general rule, there are three types of horses to avoid when screening prospects for trail events: stallions, very young horses, and highly strung horses.

Stallions tend to have fiery temperaments. They are strong and very hard to control at times. Horses like this are a menace on trail rides, when one outburst from them can disrupt a whole group of horses. This will count severely against you on any trail ride or trail class you enter, if the judge allows you in the competition at all. The judge has the right to disqualify any unruly and potentially dangerous horse. Since stallions tend to fall into this category, it is best not to choose one as a trail prospect.

Very young horses are also unsuitable for trail riding. A horse under age five may be only green broken when you buy him, and therefore may leave something to be desired in his gaits and his response to your commands. Unless you are an expert trainer, it is unwise to buy a very young horse for a trail prospect. In addition to his lack of schooling, the young horse probably has not been used much on trails, and may

This leopard-colored registered Appaloosa, SunUp Miss Six Gun, shows several qualities required of a good western trail horse. Her excellent conformation, smooth gaits, and alertness make the mare well-suited to trail events. Here her owner, Shirley Smith of Iron Moon Farm, Newbury, Massachusetts, works on "Six's" pleasure gaits in an open training field. Although very spirited, the horse moves along well on a fairly loose rein, showing she is a trustworthy trail animal.

spook easily from common trail obstacles such as water and bridges.

While young horses and stallions tend to be nervous and skittish, any other horses with this nature will not make good trail horses. Highly strung horses are unwelcome in trail classes and trail rides because their excitability makes them very unpredictable. There are too many things that may send such a horse into a frenzy, especially on a long trail ride. A horse who spooks when a leaf blows across his path may unseat his rider on a trail ride and bolt off, leaving the rider to fend for himself on the lonely trail. Trail events are hard enough without a rider having to cope with unnecessary aggravations like this, so leave the highly strung horses in the pasture and choose a more docile one for trail events.

A western trail horse should be easygoing, but not to the point of being sluggish. This can be a problem in itself, as serious as that of a high-strung horse. You should be looking for a happy medium—a horse who will go along and take commands willingly, without overdoing it. The trail horse should be alert and responsive to your every movement. When you slacken the reins a bit and apply gentle but firm pressure with both legs, he should perk up and walk along briskly. A horse who drops his head toward the ground and moves along at a snail's pace when you offer him a slack rein is not what you should be looking for in a trail horse. You need a horse who wants to work, not an old plug with no sense of competition.

On the other hand, a horse who bolts the minute you slacken the reins will not make a good trail horse either. A horse like this is more than willing; he has a mind of his own. Only a horse who will submit to the commands of the rider will make a good trail prospect.

Although many horses seem to be either one extreme or the other, some seem to be made for trail competition. These horses are not unruly and hot-tempered; neither are they lazy and sluggish. They take directions obediently and willingly. The best of these horses are at their peak when in competition. Some horses seem to know that every move counts when they are in the show ring, and they perform better before a crowd than they do in the practice ring. A horse like this is a joy to any competitive rider, for nothing is more disappointing than a horse who does beautifully in training but forgets everything you've taught him once he sets foot in the show ring.

Some horses are natural competitors and others aren't, but in order to find a proper trail horse, you have to know where to look. Obviously a training farm for Thoroughbred race horses isn't the place. Depending upon your ability as a rider, there are several likely places to look for your trail horse prospect.

Sometimes the best western trail horses are those "retired" from a ranch. Usually they are just lacking in speed and possibly in endurance. As long as you don't overwork these horses, they can do well in trail events.

Retired ranch horses are generally between 12 and 18 years old. If they have worked herding cattle on the ranch for most of their lives, they can make excellent trail horses and may also do well for you in game events. Cutting horses can maneuver well, and are used to taking their correct leads from constant turning in cattle herding.

From their use on ungroomed trails near the ranch, these horses are probably used to hilly ground and rugged terrain. They should have developed surefootedness, a quality which is essential for any good trail horse.

Generally, retired ranch horses will not shy from common trail obstacles, since they have encountered these on the trails for a decade or more. Low brush jumps shouldn't bother these horses and they can take them in stride. Ranch horses are so used to trail riding that they take to competitive events of this type naturally. These horses are quite sensible and not excitable, so they are very reliable and can make excellent trail performance horses.

However, these horses have disadvantages along with their advantages. Since they are older, they tend to be rather set in their ways. If you want to retrain a ranch horse in a particular way, you may encounter some difficulty.

In addition, you may have another problem if you are a girl or woman. Ranch horses are often accustomed to being handled and ridden by rough men, so they may not respect a new female owner. A soft voice and gentle urging just does not register on some of these horses. You may have to change your approach to get any performance from a ranch horse. Remember that he's been at this game a lot longer than you have, and he isn't about to change overnight.

Beyond this element of respect for the rider's authority, the ranch horse may be a bit too much physically for a female rider. These horses may have developed very hard mouths from rugged use. Some are at the point of having almost "no mouth" at all in terms of responding to bit pressure. A woman rider who is used to responsive and obedient mounts may not be able to cope with a hard-mouthed ranch horse, especially since she may not have strong enough arms and hands to bring response through the bit.

Unless the horse respects you and responds well to your aids, his performance in trail class will be less than commendable. Much of the judging in a trail class or a trail ride is based on obedience. Any rider who enters a horse he or she cannot handle loses points immediately with the judge. If you are riding to win, be sure you can bring immediate response from any horse you consider buying for trail competition.

While the old ranch horse may be the ideal answer for some trail competitors, he certainly is not the right horse for anyone who intends to do a lot of hard riding and showing with the same horse for many years. The retired ranch horse is being sold by the ranch because he is no longer useful to the owner. If the horse is too old to be worked as hard as the other ranch horses, he is certainly too old to be placed on a demanding training program for trail competition.

It is important to take into consideration the limitations of any horse you might buy for trail competition. All horses have limitations, no matter how great they may be in one given field. An excellent jumper may be unruly in a pleasure class, just as a fast gymkhana horse may have gaits too uncomfortable for pleasure riding. The same goes for any trail horse you consider buying. This makes the process of choosing a trail horse difficult, because you have to look for so many varied qualifications.

However, this is what makes the western trail horse so special—his versatility in many fields. Just as you have had to train yourself as a rider to compete in the varied trail events, your horse must be equally well schooled. A horse who can maneuver obstacles on the correct lead but constantly shies away from them has one attribute of a good trail horse, but his flaw cancels that out. One serious flaw is all it takes to rule out any trail horse prospect.

It may be hard to make yourself recognize a flaw when looking over a horse. It is easy to fall in love with a horse because of his conformation, smooth gaits, or particular breed you favor. But no matter how many plus factors he has, one bad trait must eliminate him from consideration if you are really serious about western trail competition. After all, trail events are highly competitive, and there is room at the top for only the very best.

Of course, your decision in purchasing a trail horse may be influenced by financial factors. Rather than buying a mediocre horse immediately, you'll do better by saving a bit longer until you can buy a good trail horse. Otherwise you'll be wasting your time and money in training a horse that has too many flaws to ever be a top trail competitor.

To avoid this obvious frustration, the trail rider should look for a horse that meets as many qualifications as he can afford. Instead of paying for a horse that is fully trained, you may be better off buying a horse who has not been used on trails, but who has characteristics that indicate he would make a good trail prospect.

Basically, you should be looking for a sound horse, between five and ten years old, who has been taught the proper gaits. Provided that he has the proper disposition, a relatively young horse can make a good trail prospect. He can be ridden as much as you want without harming his health, and will be active for many years. You will have the makings of a trail horse you can work with in training and can show successfully for many show seasons.

A good-natured horse, say about seven years old, should have had enough basic training to ready him for any intensive trail training you may want to add. He should be over the folly of his youth enough to be settled down and ready to work seriously. He is in the prime of his life, and at a perfect point to go into trail performance, both in shows and on organized rides.

Unfortunately, the fact that a horse meets the qualifications of age and disposition doesn't necessarily mean he'll make a winning trail horse. It's hard to tell until you have ridden a horse for some time and gotten to know his capabilities and natural talents, but there are some things to look for when choosing a trail horse from the general category we have described.

For example, a 7-year-old Thoroughbred may be better suited as a green hunter than as a trail horse, and a 7-year-old American Saddlebred may be better suited to performance in English Pleasure or Saddle Seat Equitation classes. Most breeds of horses can be ridden either English or western or both if properly trained, but some breeds of horses adapt more naturally to training for trail events than others.

Any horse should be used to his best advantage, and you would not want to waste a talented stadium jumper as a trail

An artist's conception of the ideal Quarter Horse illustrates why this breed is so well-suited as a trail animal. Here, artist Orren Mixer has depicted the strong, muscular build of the Quarter Horse, which provides excellent stamina on the trail. The powerful hindquarters and a strong, wide chest in the Quarter Horse really pay off in trail events, especially in endurance competitions. The alert, refined head shows the inherent intelligence of the animal, which is also important on the trail. A crazy or excitable horse is worth nothing on the trail, and actually is detrimental to the safety of all riders on the trail. Instead, a horse like this intelligent, well-built animal is what you should be looking for when you choose your western trail horse. (Photo courtesy the American Quarter Horse Assn.)

horse when his performance in trail will be only mediocre. A talented horse should be allowed to perform in the style in which he excels. That is only fair to the horse: to force him into a style for which he is not suited is wasting his talents.

Several breeds of horses adapt well to trail events, but there are a few breeds that just seem to be cut out for this type of performance. These breeds take naturally to the rugged trail events, and have been consistent winners both in the show ring and on competitive trail rides.

The typical western breeds, most commonly found on ranches out West, often make the best trail horses. Since the days of the old West, these breeds have been used on rugged mountain trails for hard day-to-day work. Through the years, the breeds have developed the traits essential for a good trail horse: surefootedness, stamina, and obedience.

Of the western breeds, the best one for trail events is usually the Quarter Horse. Although he cannot sustain long bursts of speed, as can the Thoroughbred, the Quarter Horse can endure long hours of moderately paced riding. He should have a slow jog, which will give him a good pace for resting but still moving along on timed trail rides. The Quarter Horse also has a comfortable "rocking chair" lope, which can be a good ground-covering pace for parts of the trail ride.

In addition to his gaits, the Quarter Horse is built for trail events. His conformation suits him to the rugged events. He has a wide chest and muscular legs, which give him strength. If you also use him in timed gymkhana events, the Quarter Horse makes an ideal all-around western performance horse. He is rugged enough to withstand demanding trail events, and also has the ability to pour on a burst of speed and "stop on a dime," which is essential in gymkhana events.

The Quarter Horse is known for his calm disposition and trustworthy nature. As long as he has not had a bad experience to turn him sour, the Quarter Horse can make an ideal western trail horse. Although Quarter Horses are sometimes trained as

English jumpers, they usually perform at their optimum in western trail and gymkhana events.

If it is at all possible, the best Quarter Horse investment is in a registered animal. Many horses of common stock make excellent western performance horses, but there are advantages to owning a registered horse. The registration certificate will show the horse's true age. This is important to any rider who cannot judge a horse's age from his teeth and general appearance. When you buy a registered horse there is no way the horse dealer can trick you into buying a horse that is much older than he looks.

Another benefit of owning a registered horse is that more classes in shows will be open for you to enter. Some shows have general classes for western performance horses such as trail and pleasure, but the larger shows offer classes restricted to horses of registered breeds. If you intend to do a good amount of showing with your trail horse, it may be worthwhile to save enough money to buy a registered animal.

The registration certificate may also come in handy if you buy a mare. If at any time you decide to breed her to another registered Quarter Horse, the foal will be a valuable horse. The two to three hundred dollars you pay for the stud fee will be multiplied many times after the foal is trained. Had you not bought a registered Quarter Horse mare, the foal would only be a common stock horse.

Although some common stock horses do well in trail competition, the rider with a registered animal under him knows he has something valuable to work with. A Quarter Horse with good bloodlines should possess excellent traits which your training will bring out. When you have something good to work with, the only excuse for not being a top competitor lies in the training or the rider.

So if you plan to do a lot of competing with your western trail horse, give yourself an even break to start with. Buy an animal of good stock. If you cannot buy a registered Quarter

Horse, several other breeds are well suited to trail competition.

The "color" breeds often have Quarter Horse stock in their breeding. Horses such as the Appaloosa, the Pinto, the Paint, and the Palomino are commonly used on western ranches and often have the same attributes as the Quarter Horse.

These "color" breeds are sometimes double-registered, with certificates for both the breed of their color and for their standard breed, which is usually the Quarter Horse registry. In addition to owning a registered Quarter Horse, you're also getting a horse with flashy colors. If his conformation is as striking as his color pattern, he is sure to catch the eye of any judge.

If you do buy such a horse for both his coloring and his Quarter Horse background, make sure he has good coloring. A judge will notice a poorly colored horse as much as he will a horse with excellent coloring, but the former will not gain his approval. There's no sense in buying a "color" horse with poor markings, for this will only count against you in judging. The color of the horse is less important than his ability in trail events, but it stands to reason that if you are buying a horse with a special color breed in mind, you should buy one with good, approved coloring.

One thing to watch out for in the "color" breeds is the personality of the particular horse. Sometimes stock is bred too closely, with only color results in mind, and the resulting foals are sometimes rather flighty in disposition. Some of these horses have been known to panic and run into a wall, knocking themselves and their riders down. When choosing a "color" horse, be sure to screen him carefully for any undesirable personality traits.

Other than Quarter Horses and "color" breeds with Quarter Horse background, there are not many more typical western breeds to consider for trail. Several other breeds of horses are suitable to western trail events, but most of these breeds are not basically either western or English.

Buying such a horse to train for western trail can be an advantage, at least in the training stages. A horse who will go either English or western often will adapt more easily to training for trail, since some stages of the training are best conveyed to the horse with the two-rein English method, while other parts of the training are just as easily done by Western neck reining.

One of the breeds which can make fine trail horses is the Morgan. Although Morgan classes at large horse shows are almost invariably English, with the rider in either saddle seat or park seat, more and more Morgan horses are being trained to respond to both English and western reining. It has been found that Morgans adapt well to both types of training, so the Morgan is becoming a popular alternative in western trail classes to the more common Quarter Horse types.

His willing disposition and flashy appearance have contributed toward making the Morgan a new favorite among western trail riders. A well-schooled Morgan presents a striking appearance, and his gaits reflect his proud and smooth way of going.

The Morgan's smooth gaits and the variety of gaits he can perform are a boon to any western trail rider. A Morgan horse which is trained both English and western should have two or three ways of trotting—the jog, the standard trot, and the extended trot. These three trots offer a variety that is most welcome on a long trail ride. The Morgan can use his extended trot to cover ground quickly without having to canter or lope, and can then slow down to a western jog to rest a while but still keep moving.

The Morgan's smooth gaits are an important consideration, since a trail class is marked on performance at both obstacles and pleasure gaits. Any horse must have smooth gaits if he is to be shown successfully as a western trail entry.

The western trail horse should have a slow, smooth jog which barely bounces the rider from the saddle. The jog, unlike the

English trot, is not much faster than a walk. Judges in a trail class mark strictly on the jog, so if you buy a horse trained both English and western, be sure that he can maintain a slow jog in the show ring.

Although most breeds of horses can be trained to go both English and western, not all breeds can easily master the jog. For example, Thoroughbreds often make excellent English trail horses, but probably would not do as well in a western trail class. The Thoroughbred can be good on the trail because of his endurance, speed, and jumping prowess, but he would probably be a sad sight in a western trail class show ring. The long and lanky legs of the Thoroughbred give him the ability (and the tendency) to take long strides, so he would not adapt naturally to a western jog.

Horses like this are not a good choice for western trail training. Since the Thoroughbred and other similar breeds are more suited to English riding, it is unfair to the horse to try and convert him to a way of going to which he is not naturally inclined. Always use a horse to his best advantage.

Following the same line of thinking, breeds such as the American Saddlebred also do not make likely prospects for western trail horses. These horses are traditionally schooled English, and pains are taken to perfect their five gaits. An animal like this would be wasted in western trail, and probably would not perform as well as another horse you might choose.

However, some horses that are generally trained English can make fine western trail horses. Among these are the Tennessee Walker and the Arabian. Both are flashy looking breeds, with proud carriage of head and smooth gaits. More people are beginning to train these breeds western, and have found that they adapt well. Many Walkers and Arabians have made top western trail competitors.

After deciding on the breed you feel is most suitable for western trail, it is time to begin visiting breeding farms to screen the horses you may consider buying. If you don't have the finances to buy from a breeding farm, you can begin looking at local stables.

However, if you are buying from a riding stable, it is important to really get to know the horse before you buy him. Riding school horses are notorious for having bad habits developed from being ridden day after day by new people who don't know how to ride. Watch out for nasty habits such as biting and kicking, throwing the head up to avoid bit pressure, and following whatever the horse in front does. Riding school horses often have minds of their own, and do not willingly respond to the commands of the rider. They will often test you to see if they can make you too afraid to ride them.

In the show ring, riding school horses often exhibit bad habits such as cutting corners and passing other horses too quickly. However, with enough schooling it is possible to retrain these horses. With one owner, they can become good and trustworthy mounts. If they have been used on riding stable trails, they may already have many good points of the trail horse.

A riding stable horse, or any horse for that matter, can be a pleasure to ride but very difficult to handle from the ground. A good trail horse must be gentle when mounted and when handled from the ground. He must allow a judge to handle him, must raise his hoof when asked, remain calm, and hold his hoof up until he is allowed to put it down.

This is part of every trail class, so it is important that any horse you choose for trail be gentle when handled by the judge or by you. Actually, this is an attribute that should be looked for when buying a horse for any purpose. The reasoning behind this is simple: When you're out riding on a trail and you notice your horse favoring one foot, you must immediately dismount and examine his hoof to see if anything is imbedded in it. A horse who will not allow you to lift his hoof can seriously injure his foot. As the saying goes: "no foot, no horse." It's true.

Beyond this safety factor, it is vital for the horse to be gentle when handled by the farrier. Trail horses sometimes go "barefoot," but it is a good idea to shoe them if you will be riding on hard roads or in rugged country. Any horse who will not let you touch his feet is a menace to the farrier, and some will refuse to shoe such a horse.

If you plan to use your western trail horse consistently on trail rides and in the show ring, be sure to choose one who will allow himself to be handled about the feet. If the horse is of the proper disposition and has been gradually introduced to foot handling, he should present no major problem. However, it is wise to examine the horse about his feet before you even think of buying him. You may save yourself a lot of future grief.

This is the whole point in purchasing a horse for western trail competition. You must look him over completely to be sure he fits your needs and is suitable for trail. If he meets all the qualifications that are important to you, the only thing left is to have him checked by a veterinarian for soundness. A sick animal cannot perform well, so there is no sense in buying one.

Surprisingly, the feature of a trail horse which is last in importance often comes first in the eye of the buyer. That, of course, is the horse's appearance. Everyone wants a nice looking horse, but this is not what counts on the trail. However, it may count somewhat in the show ring. Choose a handsome animal and keep him in good shape, but don't make looks your primary consideration, because the judge certainly won't.

Taking all these things into consideration, you have bought a 7- or 8-year-old western horse with a calm disposition, easy gaits, and a willing manner. Now it is time to begin his training for western trail competition.

2. *Early Training*

Since your horse will be asked to do a certain amount of railwork in the trail class, you must prepare him with training at the pleasure gaits. Your horse's early training will involve developing manners and practicing the change of gaits. He must be taught to be obedient at all times, and must master the basics like standing square and backing at your command.

Obedience is of the utmost importance in a trail class. The better your horse obeys your directions, the higher score the judge will give him.

You must train your horse thoroughly in the basics. These skills will be required in the show ring and will be necessary as background later when you teach your horse more advanced skills. The first thing you should teach your horse is to be obedient at all gaits and to switch gaits willingly. You will begin, logically, at the beginning gait—the walk.

THE WALK

To move your horse into a walk when he is standing still, press your legs gently against his sides and nudge him lightly with your heel. He should respond by going forward into a slow walk.

Although the horse will begin the walk slowly, you must perk him up. Sit deep in the saddle and pull your chest up, to indicate to the horse that you want him to walk more briskly.

If you feel him start to slow down again, nudge him with more heel. Don't allow him to plod along at a snail's pace with his head hanging to the ground.

When the horse is at a proper walk, he should feel as though

The western trail horse should walk forward smoothly and alertly, as registered Quarter Horse "Pattern In Gold" shows here.

Working with your trail horse from the ground has many added benefits. Here Conrad Smith of Iron Moon Farm, Newbury, Massachusetts, does some ground driving with Yakima Britches, a registered Appaloosa two-year-old filly. The sidechecks attached to the driving bridle put light tension on the bit, which will make the filly more receptive to a real riding bit when the time comes for her to be trained to the saddle. Working with her early from the ground helps her develop confidence in her future rider, while at the same time making her learn obedience and docility.

Work on the longe line teaches the young horse obedience and conformity in his gaits. This yearling filly, a future trail horse prospect, is Iron Moon's High Jinx, a registered Appaloosa, owned by Conrad and Shirley Smith of Iron Moon Farm, Newbury, Massachusetts.

he is going to break into a jog at any second. His head should be noticeably moving up and down, and you should be able to feel a definite forward-and-backward motion in his back.

This indicates that your horse is ready to move into a jog, but he should not do so until you give him the signal. Never allow him to change gaits whenever he pleases, or he may not obey you when it really counts—in the show ring.

The walk is a flat-footed gait with four beats. Each hoof strikes the ground separately, so you can hear a definite 1-2-3-4 rhythm. The jog is a two-beat gait, making a sound of 1-2-1-2.

THE JOG

At the jog, your horse moves on a diagonal. His front right leg and his back left leg move forward when the opposite legs are back, and vice versa. Since two legs hit the ground at one time, followed by the other two, you will hear a 1-2-1-2 rhythm.

This creates a bouncy movement, especially at the full trot. The trot and the jog are the same motion, but the jog is much slower. In an open trail class with both English and western contestants, the ring announcer will command, "Jog or trot." The English horses must trot, while the western horses must jog.

The trot is a fairly fast gait, especially for English horses who do an extended trot. In contrast, the jog is barely faster than a walk. Although the trot is very bumpy to sit, the jog is most comfortable to sit if your horse does it properly.

If your horse has not been trained to jog, he will probably have a tendency to trot at a fast clip along with the English horses. You will have to teach him to jog at the proper speed, or he will never take ribbons for you in a western trail class.

It can be difficult to train a horse to jog while mounted. When you ask your horse to jog, he will continue to trot until he has learned better. Your tendency will probably be to pull on the reins to get the horse to slow down into a jog. This will not bring the response you desire from your horse. You will

The jog is a slow, two-beat gait. Here, professional trainer Bob Webster puts Pattern In Gold into a smooth western jog.

have signaled him to trot (as far as he knows), and then pulled back on the reins. To your horse, this means you wanted him to trot but that you changed your mind and now want him to walk. This is the only way he can interpret your actions since he does not understand what a jog is yet.

You can avoid this confusion in the horse if you teach him to jog from the ground. Try it first with your horse in a halter and lead rope.

Take the length of the lead rope in your left hand, holding it with your right hand just under the horse's chin. Walk to the left of him, right beside his head. Never let him walk ahead of you, for that is not the proper way to lead a horse.

As you give the verbal command to "Walk," pull gently on the rope under the horse's chin and begin to walk beside him. After you have walked about five yards, say "Trot!" in a crisp voice, and begin to run slowly. You should be just about running in place, slowly moving ahead. This will teach your horse that "Trot!" means you want him to jog.

Using the word "trot" will not confuse your horse later. There is no reason for you to teach him to do a full trot, for he can already do it on his own. He will never be asked to trot in the show ring as long as you continue to ride him western.

The only instance when you may want your horse to do a fast trot is on a trail ride, when you are competing against a time clock. In that case, all you will have to do is give your horse a kick when he is jogging, and he will move into a full trot. You won't need to give him a verbal command, so there is no way he can confuse jogging and trotting from your use of the word "trot."

When you are teaching your horse to jog on a lead rope, hold the rope taut under his chin. Pull it slightly back and up under his head, so he will be forced to carry his head high and keep his chin tucked in.

If your horse has his neck stretched way out in front of him and his head hanging down, he cannot do a proper jog. Although the jog is slow in terms of covering ground, it requires quick action in the horse's legs. His legs move up and down quickly, but they do not stretch out far in front so he cannot travel very fast. In order to perform such a quick movement, your horse must be collected and alert.

When you ask your horse to jog beside you as you lead him, he may just do a fast walk. When the horse has not yet learned the jog, he only knows the walk and the full trot. He may feel you are running too slowly for him to trot beside you—and he is right. You are running slowly to get him to jog.

If he insists on walking, start to run faster until he trots. Then slow down, constantly repeating "trot-trot, trot-trot," to make sure he doesn't slow down into a walk.

Avoid making a "cluck-cluck" noise as many riders do to get their horses to jog or trot. If you do this in the training process, your horse may come to rely on it as a signal to jog. You should never make such noises in the show ring, so don't make them while training your horse.

You may have to practice having your horse jog on a lead rope for several weeks before he really gets the hang of it. If he has been taught to lunge, put him on a lunge line next and see if he will still jog properly for you. By now he should no longer need you running beside him to set the speed of the jog.

If he does well on the lunge, your horse should be able to jog properly with you mounted. Hop up, ask him to walk, and then kick him gently with both heels.

Your horse should move right into a jog. If he walks instead, that means he was not ready yet. Urge him into a brisk walk, and then try asking him to jog again.

If your horse breaks into a trot, pull gently on the reins and say "trot-trot" quietly. That should slow him down into a jog, without making him go all the way back into a walk.

Enough practice should see your horse performing well at a jog. Once he has mastered it, you can begin work at the lope.

THE LOPE

The lope will require more training than the jog, since there are more things your horse will have to learn at this gait. He will have to learn to begin the lope from a walk without inserting the jog as a transition gait, and he will also have to learn to take leads at the lope.

The lope is a three-beat gait in which one of the horse's front legs reaches out further and slightly before the other leg (see illustration). The leg which reaches out in front is said to be leading. In a right lead, for example, the right leg is reaching out the furthest.

Getting your horse to take the correct lead is not a simple matter. Many untrained riders can get their horses to go from a jog to a lope, but cannot make their mounts take a lope from a walk. By using the proper aids to signal for one lead or the other, you can make your horse break into a lope from any gait, and on the correct lead.

Your body position and weight shift will have a great deal to do with making your horse take his proper lead. If you want your horse to take a right lead, you must get him to concentrate on his right side. Your reins will direct him to the right, as you lay them across the left side of his neck.

By neck reining, you have gotten your horse ready to either change from a left lead to a right lead, or to start loping from a walk with a right lead. Your legs will do the rest of the work. Touch the horse behind the cinch with your left heel while keeping most of your weight in the right stirrup, which should be slightly ahead of the cinch. This will give your horse impulsion toward the left, and should get him to go right into a right lead. Practice making your horse take right and left leads from the walk or from a standstill. Later you will practice changing leads while already at the lope in what is called the flying change of leads.

The lope is a rocking, three-beat gait. A horse like Pattern In Gold is a pleasure to ride at the lope. She is the World Champion Western Riding Horse.

THE FLYING CHANGE OF LEADS

One way of changing leads which is particularly effective for western horses, especially in gymkhana games, is called the flying change of leads. It is important for any trail horse to be able to do a flying change of leads, for he may be asked to do so in a western trail class. This takes a lot of practice for both horse and rider, but it is a skill well worth learning.

The best way to prepare for practicing the change of leads is to lope your horse in a wide circle. If you can use the local riding ring for practice, you can ride at the rail for a circle. If not, ride circles in an open field.

Circling is a good maneuver, because later it will give your horse a reason to change leads. When he is loping a circle to the left, he should be using the left lead; when you change direction and circle to the right, he will have to change to the right lead.

If there are poles or trees spaced widely apart in the field, you can use these to ride around when you want to change directions and leads. You can also put your own obstacles out to circle around, such as tires or barrels. These will come in handy during the training process.

To get your horse to change his leads, try riding toward an obstacle in a circular motion to the left, with your horse on a left lead. As you approach the obstacle, you should ready your horse to turn around it; this means having him collected and alert.

Give the aids for a right lead just when your horse gets behind the obstacle and before he starts to turn around it. He should change leads immediately and continue around the obstacle in a circular motion, this time to the right (see diagram).

What you are attempting to do is to make your horse take a change of leads while he is running straight ahead, not during a turn. It is easier and more natural for a horse to make the change while turning, for the turn gives him a reason to change his leads. However, the judge wants to see the horse

The flying change of leads is a complex skill to teach a horse, but Pattern In Gold illustrates the change here with skill. (Photo by R. A. Greene, DVM)

make the change of leads at your direction and whenever you want him to. One good way to practice this is to ride a figure eight.

FIGURE EIGHTS

The figure eight is a common pattern in athletic events. It is a graceful motion which requires the athlete to continue an action while changing direction, without losing his balance. Ice skaters practice figure eights constantly. Since riding is as graceful a sport as skating, you should practice them too.

If you have been practicing the change of leads from a circle, your horse will take naturally to the figure eight pattern. The figure eight is actually two separate circles, joined together for a short distance (see diagram).

Many riders mistakenly ride a figure eight in more of the pattern used in barrel racing—as part of a clover leaf, with the two circles connected at only one point (see diagram). When making this type of figure eight, the horse has to change leads while changing direction into the second part of the figure eight. This is not what the judge wants you to do. He expects you to ride a round circle, and then have your horse change leads while running straight for the short distance where the two circles meet. When your horse reaches the rounded part of the other circle, he should already have changed his lead.

To get your horse to change his lead while running on a straight path, give him the aids to change the lead as soon as you come out of the last rounded part of the circle. That way he should make the change right at the middle point between the two circles, and should take the next circle on the proper lead.

This takes a lot of practice to perfect, of course. Your horse probably won't have too much trouble with the change of leads, but he will need practice in riding full, rounded circles and finding the middle point to change leads.

You will also need practice here, for it is the rider who de-

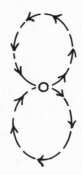

Most people visualize the Figure Eight as a loose figure of the number "8." This pattern is correct, in that the two round parts of the figure touch at only one point. However, this is not exactly what the judge is looking for in a Figure Eight.

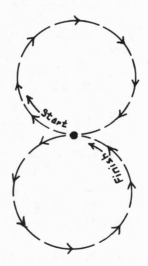

Instead, the judge wants to see two even, perfect circles which touch at one point in their exact centers. This diagram still resembles the number "8," but in a more perfect form than we are often used to seeing it.

cides how to cut the circles and where to make the horse turn. Try to make your circles as full and even as possible, for the judge will be watching for this. When you start, you may want to mark off even circles in the dirt where you are riding. After enough practice, you should be able to judge for yourself where an even circle lies.

Try to do this maneuver as evenly and smoothly as you can. When two riders are tied for first place in a trail class even after the obstacle competition, the judge will sometimes ask each to ride a figure eight, since this is a quick way to decide who is better. The blue ribbon will go to the rider whose horse does the best figure eight, so it is worthwhile for you to practice until your horse can do it smoothly.

HALTING

Now that your horse can make a change of leads and can go from a walk to a lope, he must learn to do the reverse. Getting a horse to halt from a lope correctly is something you should practice for performance in western trail classes.

Many horses have the tendency to "go down through the gears" when coming to a stop. Instead of going right from a lope to a halt, they will insert transitions, such as the trot and jog. This is easier and more natural for the horse, but you must teach him to do otherwise.

If you consider the halt as a gait, you can incorporate training to halt with a general training of the horse to change various gaits. He should be able to go from any movement to any other, with no steps in between. This includes the halt as well as the other gaits.

For example, the ring announcer in trail class may ask for this series of gaits: walk, lope, jog, halt, jog, walk, lope, reverse direction, jog, lope, halt. Your horse should have no problem doing any of these changes if you have practiced them with him.

You can have your horse practice the change of gaits while

on your daily pleasure ride. Don't ask him to change too many times, or he may get tired of the frequent changes. Every once in a while, ask your horse to change from one gait to another without putting in a transition gait.

As long as you give him the proper signal for each gait, he should respond in the correct manner. If he does not, try it again. When he finally does what you want, praise him verbally so he'll know it's worthwhile obeying you.

To get him to halt from any gait, shift your weight as far back as possible in the saddle and sit deep. Pull back on the reins (not too hard) with steady pressure, then relax the reins when you feel your horse slow down.

You may want to say "whoa" when asking your horse to halt if he already knows the word. Don't use it every time, for you should not use any verbal commands in the show ring. After enough practice, your horse should come to a halt whenever you ask him to.

This training to halt and to change gaits will be a long and constant process. By doing this on your pleasure rides, you will be keeping your horse in practice for the show ring. If you do it a little every day, you won't have to set aside special training sessions for the change of gaits and the halt.

BACKING

Once your horse has halted, you may want him to back up. In any case, backing is a very important skill for the horse to learn. It can mean the difference between safety and serious injury, especially for a western trail horse.

Your horse may walk into something dangerous on the trail. Perhaps he has walked halfway across a railroad track, and then you notice fragments of glass between the railroad ties. Since you don't want him to walk any further into the glass, you'll want your horse to back out of the danger.

Because backing can be so vital, many judges will ask you to back your horse in a trail class. Once the horse learns to back he will always know how, so it is certainly worth training him to back.

Many horses respond well to the verbal command "back, back" as a mounted rider pulls the reins back, keeping the horse's head tucked and low. But if your horse doesn't know what "back" means, you'll have to teach him from the ground.

This is a rather simple thing to teach your horse, compared to some of the more advanced skills he has already learned. From the ground, you can stand in front of him and push on his chest, saying "back." When he takes a step back, praise him. That will teach him what "back" means and will make him enjoy doing it.

Then you can mount again and try to make your horse back. It shouldn't take him long to get the idea. If he does have trouble learning to back, try using two hands on the reins. He may back more easily if you lightly "seesaw" on his mouth by pulling one rein and then the other.

After he can back well, you'll only need to practice backing him every few weeks or so. Horses have good memories, and infrequent reinforcement of this skill will be sufficient.

STANDING SQUARE

The only other skill your horse will be asked to exhibit in trail class which falls under the category of early training is to stand square.

While English horses are taught to stretch, western horses are only expected to stand square. The term "standing square" is self-explanatory. It means that the horse is standing with his four feet evenly placed, so that if you drew a line between them, it would form a square.

When your horse is standing square, the judge will be looking him over for conformation and grooming. Choose a flat spot for him to stand. Don't make the horse stand on a hill, even if it is only a slight incline. A slope will make your horse look unbalanced and maybe swaybacked.

Backing is a skill every western trail horse should know. In addition to being necessary for show ring performance, backing properly can come in very handy when confronted with a problem obstacle on the trail.

Standing square is an important skill to teach your horse for performing in trail classes at horse shows. When viewed from the side, a horse standing perfectly square will appear to have only two legs, for the others are in exact line with them on the other side.

To get him "squared up," lead your horse forward and then back him step by step until he is standing square. By moving one step at a time, you can stop your horse when all his feet are even. Often only one of his feet will be out of line, and you'll just have to get him to move back until that foot is even with the rest.

While he is standing square, your horse should hold his head high and should look alert. This will add to the judge's favorable impression. Every little thing counts in a horse show, so be sure to make everything work in your favor.

Once your horse has mastered the basics of his training as a western trail horse, you can begin his training for the other part of the trail class—the obstacle course. Many of the basic skills he has already learned will be vital for good performance at the obstacles, so the time you have spent on his training will be rewarded.

Bob Webster, on Pattern In Gold, with the horse standing square, as shown from the front view.

3. The Gate Obstacle

The gate obstacle is standard in any good trail class. Like any other trail obstacle, the gate is there for two reasons—it serves as a good test of several skills a trail horse must know, and it is an obstacle commonly encountered on a trail ride.

Riders may gripe at having to prepare for the gate obstacle in western trail classes, but the training is worthwhile. Great emphasis is placed on the gate in judging, for it is an important part of the trail class.

Just as other tasks in the trail class are based on their importance on the trail, the gate must be mastered for any trail ride. Being able to open and close a gate from horseback is an essential part of trail riding etiquette. Beyond that, it is functional. This skill can save you time against the clock that you would waste if you dismounted to open and close the gate.

The gate obstacle serves as an excellent test of both horse and rider, and of the two as a team. In order to execute the opening and closing of the gate smoothly, three factors are required:

a trained horse, a knowledgeable rider, and a fine coordination between the horse and the rider.

This obstacle is a demanding one. It requires a great amount of agility on the part of both horse and rider. The horse must maneuver himself at an odd angle to the gate and stay as close as possible so the rider can reach the latch. The rider must in turn do his part for the horse and open and close the gate without letting it strike his mount.

The task requires much cooperation between horse and rider. It is an awkward thing to attempt, and even more awkward to master, but it can be accomplished through training and practice.

Your job in training may be made harder or easier by your horse. Some horses take better to training for the gate obstacle than others. The hardest of all to train are horses who are afraid of the gate.

If your horse is afraid of the gate, you will have to concentrate on overcoming his fear before you can hope to teach him anything. A little apprehension at first sight of the obstacle is natural, but most horses quell their fears after they become accustomed to the gate. Once the horse knows the gate won't harm him, he should take to the training willingly.

One way to ensure that your horse won't be afraid of the gate is to act fully confident around him and the gate. Don't anticipate any fear in your horse, or you may create it. Horses are constantly on their guard, and are quick to notice any apprehension in the rider.

Just as a horse usually refuses a jump because he senses his rider's nervousness, a trail horse may become balky at the gate obstacle if he senses any apprehension in his rider. You know the gate is harmless, and you should have no problem training your horse for the gate if you convey this feeling to him.

How you handle the gate will also affect your horse's attitude toward it. Horses don't like swinging obstacles, and they may fear that the gate will swing open and hit them. Chances of the horse fearing this are lessened if you always open the gate slowly and close it securely. Don't allow the wind to catch the gate and send it banging. It only takes one bad experience to ruin a good horse. All your efforts can go down the drain if you allow an accident at the gate to frighten or harm your horse.

As rider and trainer, you are largely responsible for any attitude your horse develops toward the gate obstacle. If the training is a pleasant experience for your horse, he will offer no objection to performing at the gate in a trail class. Your attitude will be reflected by your horse, so it is important that you begin training with a good attitude toward the project.

If you regard training as a new and enjoyable venture, your horse will too. Horses, like people, become bored with the same old routine. No horse likes to be ridden over the same trail on every ride, and he does not like to do the same practice for shows over and over. Your horse will welcome the chance to learn something new like the gate obstacle as long as you keep your spirits high during all phases of the training.

However, while a positive attitude is necessary in training, there is such a thing as being overly enthusiastic. Too many novice trainers overdo it in the excitement of teaching their horse a new skill. It is important not to push your horse too hard in training.

Give your horse a break once in a while during a training session. Stop the lesson for a while and take a nice long trail ride. This will refresh both you and your horse, and should help him go back to the lessons again. Remember, training for one specific trail obstacle such as the gate can become as boring to your horse as any other routine.

Keeping this in mind, you should realize you cannot expect to see immediate results in the early stages of the training. Training is a long process, especially when preparing for western trail events. You only defeat your own purpose by hurrying.

Taking the training step by step is especially important in preparing for the gate obstacle. Most other trail obstacles require the mastery of only one skill; some require no skill and just the courage to pass the obstacle. The gate obstacle, unlike many others, requires the horse to be expert at three difficult skills—the turn on the haunches, the turn on the forehand, and the sidepass.

THE TURN ON THE HAUNCHES

Performing the gate obstacle requires a most gymnastic horse. The first step he must master is the turn on the haunches, which requires him to support his weight fully on his hindquarters while turning his front end in a wide arc.

In order to teach a horse such a skill, you will have to do your training in an area which offers few distractions. If you train at a spot where your horse can see his stablemates out grazing and frolicking, he is sure to watch them instead of paying attention to your directions. It is asking too much to expect a horse to learn trail skills unless you use a work area where he can concentrate on the task at hand.

The best place to work is one where you can isolate your horse from the other horses in the corral or pasture. An indoor riding ring is ideal. The show ring is not a good training area for the gate obstacle because you are looking for a corner to use.

The corner is excellent for early training in skills like the turn on the haunches for two reasons. It discourages the horse from stepping backward while doing the turn, and it also keeps him from turning too far.

Both of these factors are important in performing the gate obstacle in the show ring. If the horse steps backward, he may set himself off balance. If he turns too far, he may not end up at the correct distance from the gate.

In performing this obstacle in the show ring, the horse needs only to make a quarter turn on the haunches. The corner is perfect for teaching the quarter turn on the haunches because it only allows the horse to make a 90-degree turn. Later, after the horse has mastered the quarter turn, you can go on to half turns and then to a full 360-degree circle turn. However, when teaching the turn on the haunches, a corner will be wide enough to teach the quarter turn.

When performing the turn on the haunches, the horse anchors his hindquarters to support a wide turn by his front end. His back legs remain in place, pivoting slightly to aid the motion of the turn. His front legs lift up from the ground and swing from one edge of the corner to the other.

While some trail training is done from the ground, the turn on the haunches is taught mounted. The rider sits deep, with his weight toward the back of the saddle. This is important, because the rider's weight tends to steady the horse's hindquarters and discourage him from stepping forward.

During this training, the rider's hands are kept low, over the horse's withers. Although you will be using a western saddle, it is best to use an English snaffle bridle while teaching the turn on the haunches. It is easier to direct the horse with the two-hand English method, and it also helps him understand what you want him to do. Holding the reins in two hands, try to keep your hands low.

To begin the training for the turn on the haunches, position your horse so the pointed part of the corner is behind him. Edge your horse over as close as possible to the right-hand side, along the fence posts. This gives you plenty of room to work with, and has you prepared to begin instruction for a turn on the haunches to the left.

In executing this turn to the left, the directing is done with left aids. To begin the turn, pull the left rein slightly to guide the horse's head to the left. This will send him in the general direction you want him to turn. Once his head starts to turn left, his body will naturally follow in order to maintain his balance.

While you direct his head with your left hand, keep your left leg firm at the horse's side near the cinch. The leg pressure helps steady the horse's hindquarters and will keep him from following any tendency to move his back feet.

Although your left hand and leg are actually doing the directing, your right aids also play a part in teaching the turn on the haunches. The right hand must remain low, and it is important to keep that hand back over the withers because it helps the horse keep his weight back on the haunches. If you keep your hands forward or lean forward, the horse will tend to do the same. The turn on the haunches cannot be accomplished unless the horse's weight remains in his hindquarters.

While the right hand helps keep the weight back, the rider's right leg helps keep the horse from turning his hind end to the right. The right leg should stay a few inches behind the cinch to help steady the horse and to keep his back legs planted firmly on the ground.

Keeping all this in mind, you can begin your horse's training for the turn on the haunches at any time. Remember to use your four aids at the same time and to apply pressure as evenly as possible. If your left leg pushes too hard on the horse's side in the turn to the left, he may become confused: your hands are pulling him to the left, but your leg is pushing him to the right. In order to avoid this confusion, apply the aids evenly and at the same time.

If you keep your weight back and use the aids properly, your horse should take one step to the left when you begin to pull the left rein. Once he takes the step, relax any pressure you have been applying. Reward the horse with verbal praise, and ask him to take another step in the same direction. Wait a few moments between each step, but ask him to repeat the step until he has turned on his haunches all the way from the right side of the fence to the left.

If your horse responds correctly to your directions, stop his training for the day. Do not ask him to complete a full quarter turn on the haunches the first day. Repeat the instruction for a short period of time each day, until the horse understands that you want him to make one quick turn from the right side of the fence to the left.

It is a good idea to vary the turn from right to left and from left to right. Horses are creatures of habit, and if you train for one week on a left turn the horse may balk when you try to make him turn to the right. Don't confuse the horse by changing the direction of the turn at every other try, but do allow some variety so he will not favor one side or the other.

By daily practice, your horse should learn the turn on the haunches within a few weeks. If he is not responding in the manner you expect him to, it means you are doing something wrong. A judge always goes by the rule that if a horse does not perform in the correct way, it is not the animal's fault but the fault of the rider. You are responsible for conveying a message to the horse. If he does not obey, he is probably not interpreting it correctly because you are confusing him.

If you are having difficulty teaching your horse the turn on the haunches, check your position in the saddle and your use of the aids. Most problems stem from incorrect use of the aids, since they are your means of communicating with the horse. Once you apply the aids smoothly and correctly, your horse will eventually respond. It may take time, but time is the name of the game in training for western trail performance.

When your horse understands what you expect of him and can perform the turn on the haunches in the 90-degree angle of the fence corner, take him out of the corner and try it in the open. Your horse may have a tendency to step forward or backward here, since there is no fence behind him to discourage such movement. Now you must depend solely on the aids to make the horse respond correctly. It is important that your horse practice out in the open, for there will be no fence in the show ring for him to turn in.

After the horse has mastered the turn on the haunches you

will have to discard the snaffle bit you've been using for the training. Now that the horse knows what you expect of him, you should go back to using his western bridle and bit. Try neck reining the horse, and see if he will still do a turn on the haunches. If you have trained him well for the turn, and if he is used to being ridden both English and western, you should have no trouble.

When your horse is performing a 90-degree turn on the haunches with full confidence, going in both directions, and using neck reining, you can move on to 180-degree and full 360-degree turns. Those are optional, since they aren't really necessary to perform the gate obstacle. But they can be valuable on the trail and in other events, and if you are interested in having your horse learn these larger turns it may be worth your while.

Now that your horse has mastered the turn on the haunches, you are ready to go on to the next step in preparing for the gate obstacle: the turn on the forehand.

THE TURN ON THE FOREHAND

Your horse should pick up the turn on the forehand easily, since it is similar to the turn on the haunches. The turn on the forehand is just the opposite of the turn on the haunches, but it involves the same types of movements.

In this turn, different parts of the horse's body are working than those in the turn on the haunches. This new turn involves the horse anchoring his front quarters and pivoting on them, while his hindquarters lift from the ground to make a wide arc turn.

Unlike the turn on the haunches, this turn can initially be taught from the ground. Position yourself at the point of the corner, with your horse facing you.

You may have an easier time teaching your horse the turn on the forehand because the training involves a very natural response from the horse. You will apply pressure on his side, and can expect him to move away from it. This is the natural tendency of the horse to maintain balance, and luckily that is exactly what you want him to do here.

If you've ever gone into a straight stall to feed and had the horse lean all his weight on you, you have probably already done something similar to the training you'll be giving him for the turn on the forehand. When the horse leans on you and presses you against the side of the stall, your reaction is to push back on his side. When you do this, it pushes his center of balance to the other side. His body leans that way, and his feet follow to maintain his balance.

This is just about what you'll be doing in the early training for the turn on the haunches, with one exception—you don't want your horse to take a step with his front feet. His front quarters must remain firm on one spot on the ground during the turn. They move slightly, but only in a pivoting move. The horse must not move his front feet from the ground at any time during this turn.

In order to keep the horse from moving his front feet, keep his head toward you. You may even have to pull his head a bit, to help him get the idea of keeping his front quarters steady. When you pull the horse's head toward you the entire front half of his body shifts its balance toward the front, and this is what must happen if the horse is to learn to execute the turn on the forehand.

At the same time you are pulling the horse's head toward you, apply pressure on the horse's side, pushing his hindquarters away from you. A long crop may be necessary if you are to reach back far enough on the horse's side.

If you do this movement smoothly, the horse should respond by taking one step with his hindquarters. However, the horse may tend to shift his front feet in the early training. If he does, pull his head even closer to you. With the head leaning far enough in the opposite direction of the turn, the horse cannot move his front quarters without setting himself off balance, and this should cure any movement of his front quarters.

After your horse has learned to take one step the correct way, the rest of the training is similar to the pattern for teaching the turn on the haunches. Ask him for just one step at a time at first, gradually increasing the steps until he can make one smooth move. The corner will help you here since it will keep the horse from turning too far in the early stages of the training.

Once the horse can take a few steps this way, you can try the whole thing again, this time mounted. In turning to the left, you will pull the horse's head around slightly with the right rein while you apply pressure with your left leg. The left rein and the right leg are used to steady the horse in these moves.

You will probably have more success in the beginning if you use the two-handed English reining method. This will be necessary if you need to pull the horse's head around often to convey the idea that he should not move his front quarters. After he understands this, you should revert to your western bridle since you'll be using it in the show ring.

Now that your horse has learned both the turn on the haunches and the turn on the forehand, you can offer some variety in the training sessions. Although you are now concentrating on teaching the horse the turn on the forehand, go back and review the turn on the haunches once in a while. Trying to teach a horse two things at the same time is bad, but there is nothing wrong with occasionally going back to review something he has already learned. This will give him some variety and keep him refreshed so he won't forget what you've already taught him.

After the horse is doing turns on the forehand and turns on the haunches confidently and skillfully, you are ready to go on to the third phase of training for the gate obstacle. Your horse must now learn to sidepass.

Mastering the sidepass is vital for competing at the gate obstacle in a western trail class in shows. Here, SunUp Miss Six Gun takes her first step to initiate the sidepass. The mare's ears are turned backward not because she is being obstinate, but because she is listening to the encouraging words of her rider-owner, Shirley Smith of Iron Moon Farm, Newbury, Massachusetts. This horse is so well-schooled that Shirley has her practice the sidepass in an open training field, instead of in the corner of a corral as suggested for beginners.

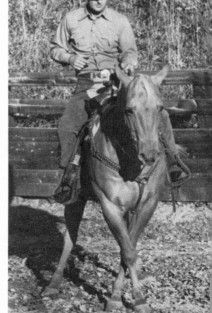

Here, Bob Webster on Pattern In Gold illustrates the sidepass.

THE SIDEPASS

Although the sidepass involves the horse moving sideways in an even motion, the simplest way to teach him this move is to have him move his front quarters first, followed by his hindquarters. After the horse has had enough practice, he should be able to incorporate these two moves into a smooth motion.

The sidepass can be easily taught while mounted, but you may want to try one thing before you mount. To give the horse the general idea that you want him to move sideways, push him gently on the side while you stand at his side. When he takes a step sideways, reward him with verbal praise.

With the idea of moving sideways fresh in your horse's mind, you may now mount and try to effect the same result. A corner may again be useful to keep the horse from stepping forward, but the horse will eventually have to learn to sidepass without the corner and fenceposts.

If you are using a corner, have the horse face it. To begin the sidepass to the left, pull the horse's head slightly to the left while applying pressure near the cinch with your right leg.

This should cause the horse to take a step to the left with his front feet. It may be just as easy for you to teach this by neck reining; if not, you can use the English snaffle again. It is best to try it first with a western bit and bridle, and see if the horse responds in the correct way to neck reining. If he does not, revert to the English bit and two-handed reining until he understands. Then go back to your western tack.

When the horse has taken his first step to the left with his front feet, stop a moment, then move your right leg behind the cinch and apply pressure. This should cause the horse to move his hindquarters just as he moved his front ones. After taking a step with the front quarters and then a step with the rear quarters, the horse should be standing square as if he had never moved.

Once your horse has taken these two steps in succession, he has just about mastered the whole idea of the sidepass. The only thing left to do here is to practice the movements until the horse is moving smoothly sideways. The best trail horses look as though they are moving their front and rear quarters simultaneously during the sidepass, although an action this smooth will take long hours of training and practice.

Just as in teaching the turn on the haunches and the turn on the forehand, don't overwork your horse while teaching him to sidepass. Turning can be interesting for a horse, but walking sideways can be pretty boring, on top of being an unnatural way for him to move. So be patient; he'll learn.

Now that your horse has mastered the three basic steps necessary for competing at the gate obstacle in a trail class, it is time to link the three movements into a logical pattern.

THE GATE OBSTACLE

Before you attempt to teach your horse the gate obstacle, be sure he is fully acquainted with the gate you'll be using for the training. Let him walk up to the gate and sniff it; then open and close the gate gently to show your horse that it won't harm him.

You will probably have no trouble at all with the gate obstacle if your horse has a gate in his paddock. However, if he has never seen a gate, this obstacle may confuse and frighten the horse. Take it gently: if you have to spend a week acquainting your horse with the gate, do so. Nothing can be taught to a horse when any element of fear or mistrust exists.

Before you work your horse through the gate, you should go through the motions in open space. Practice your two turns and the sidepass in various combinations. Don't turn the horse too much or you may make him dizzy, but do practice the three different movements, and be sure your horse can link them together before you try him at the gate obstacle.

When your horse is completing these movements smoothly, you may attempt the gate. You may want to lead him from the ground through the gate first, so that he will get used to the

This series of photos shows Bob Webster riding veteran show horse Pattern In Gold through the gate obstacle, going forward.

This series of photos shows Bob Webster taking Pattern In Gold through the gate obstacle, with the procedure reversed. Instead of going forward through the obstacle, he takes the mare backward through it.

idea of walking through it. Then you can mount and ask him to use his knowledge of the two turns and the sidepass to get you both through the gate.

Do not ride right up to the gate when you start. Position yourself parallel to the gate, several feet away from it. Give the aids for your horse to sidepass up to the gate, and stop him when he is close enough for you to reach the latch.

Some horses may favor one side or the other in lining themselves up beside the gate. If your horse does have such a preference, it is permissible to allow it, as long as you don't mind which side of the gate you start from. As a confident rider, it shouldn't matter to you.

When you are close enough, reach out and unlatch the gate. While opening the gate, ask your horse to do a quarter turn on the haunches. This is necessary if he is to pass through the gate

This alert and intelligent Arabian is a sure winner, shown here in his show ring competition at the gate obstacle, passing smoothly and confidently through it. The horse is registered Arabian Rafsit, who is a U.S. Top Ten Champion Arabian Trail Horse and also a U.S. Champion National Arabian Stock Horse. He was the 1973 AHSA High Point Arabian Gelding. Anyone with the luck to own a horse like this should be a consistent winner in trail events. (Photo courtesy the International Arabian Horse Assn.)

smoothly; otherwise he would have to move around awkwardly until his front quarters were in the proper position to allow him to pass through.

Keeping your hand on the gate at all times, ride through to the other side. Now your horse's front quarters will be heading away from the latch end of the gate, so you will have to ask him to do a quarter turn on the forehand to straighten himself out.

This turn should again place the horse parallel to the gate so that you can sidepass up to it and close the latch. That is all there is to completing the gate obstacle in a trail class or on a trail ride.

Sounds simple? It is, as long as both horse and rider are trained to work together as a team. This is what the judge will be watching for, so it is worthwhile to practice the gate often before a show in order to develop coordination between you and your horse.

If your horse knows his two turns and the sidepass, and can link them well, you should have no trouble perfecting your performance at the gate obstacle. In capsule form, the steps are:

1. Position horse parallel to gate.
2. Sidepass up to latch.
3. Pull latch and open gate.
4. Do quarter turn on haunches.
5. Ride through to other side of gate.
6. Do quarter turn on forehand.
7. Sidepass up to gate.
8. Close latch and gate.

The gate obstacle is one of the most difficult to master since it involves much agility on the part of the horse, and this is why it is weighted so highly in judging a western trail class. However, by breaking the task down into three linked movements, teaching a horse to master the gate obstacle can be done more easily than most suspect.

Competing at the gate obstacle requires a great amount of practice in order to perfect the required skills. Here, a rider in the show ring begins to unlatch the gate before her horse passes through it. (Photo courtesy of the American Quarter Horse Assn.)

It may take months to fully master the gate obstacle, but once completed, the training is very worthwhile. Not only do you have a horse who can perform one of the most difficult trail tasks well, but you also have an agile horse who can make skilled turns. This knowledge may come in handy some day on a trail ride when your horse is in a situation where he has to do a turn on the haunches or a turn on the forehand.

A horse who does not know these turns may harm himself when caught in such a situation on the trail. There are times when you want the horse to move one part of his body without shifting the other half. In this case, a horse who does not know the turns will probably step with both feet. This move could prove disastrous if he has become entangled in something, so training your horse for the gate obstacle has more benefits than just in the show ring.

In addition, the moves used for the gate obstacle are the same ones used for some other trail class obstacles. Now that your horse has learned to adapt these moves to the gate, he can easily be trained to use them in other obstacle situations. The turn on the haunches, the turn on the forehand, and the sidepass can be the three most valuable moves your trail horse will ever learn.

4. Other Obstacles

While the gate is the most highly judged obstacle in a western trail class, there are several other standard obstacles that your horse will be asked to perform. It is important to prepare him for all the obstacles because good performance at the gate will not cancel out poor performance at the other obstacles. A trail class is designed to test your horse as an all around trail mount, so the judge will expect him to do well at all the obstacles. Remember that the trail horse is supposed to be versatile and adaptable to any trail situation, and should be able to handle any obstacle the judge might think up.

The various obstacles are set up to test your horse's courage and agility, and several are designed purely to see if they can frighten your horse. Since horses spook easily from objects they are unfamiliar with, you must prepare your mount for all the obstacles he might possibly be asked to negotiate in a trail class.

This training will come in handy later on competitive trail rides. While some of the obstacles in a trail class are uncommon ones, most are the type of thing your horse will encounter on the trail. The others are representative of real objects which may frighten the horse on the trail.

Why is such an emphasis placed on testing the horse's nerves? The answer is simple. A wooded trail holds many surprises which can frighten almost any horse, but a good trail horse will not spook from these things. To keep himself and his rider from being injured, the trail horse must obey the rider even when he is afraid of something on the trail path. The horse must trust his rider enough to obey his directions at all times.

Only the best western trail horses will give their riders this trust, and that is why trail competition is so keen. It requires a lot of training and practice to get your horse to traverse frightening obstacles with confidence. Your horse has to learn to trust you as a rider before he can overcome any fear he may have of a given obstacle.

If you have a nervous horse, you may be in for quite a long training time in order to prepare him for the trail class obstacles. You would be much better off with a calm horse, because it will be much easier to teach him to perform these obstacles. This is why disposition is so important in choosing a trail horse. If you overlooked this factor and have bought a skittish horse, you may have a handful in training him for trail obstacles.

One problem with a nervous horse is that he may be too unpredictable around the obstacles. A skittish horse is ruled by moods and instincts. If he has a calm day, he may perform the obstacles without hesitation. On another day, when the wind is blowing strongly enough to frighten him, the horse may refuse the same obstacle and act as though he has never seen it.

You never know how a horse of this nature is going to react to an obstacle in the show ring or on the trail ride. This unreliability makes the horse a poor trail prospect, and a judge will be quick to notice his undesirable traits.

If you have gone ahead and bought a flighty horse for trail

events, don't despair. There are ways to train such animals. The training will require extra patience on your part, and may take much longer than it would have with a calmer horse. If your horse is suited to trail performance except for his nervousness, you can end up with a competent trail entry if you work at the training hard enough.

Dedication to the task at hand will be vital on your part as trainer. You must never lose your temper, especially with a nervous horse. This may require considerable self-restraint on your part, since a skittish horse can be very trying at times.

When your horse shies from an obstacle for no apparent reason, your immediate reaction may be to punish him—but this is the worst thing you can do. You must remain calm and patient when the horse becomes excitable or you'll never teach him anything.

Remember, you must set an example for your horse. If you take his antics with calmness and patience, he should begin to settle down. On the other hand, if you react with a burst of temper you are sure to make the horse even more excitable than he was to start with.

Unless you have a patient nature, you may find yourself becoming too frustrated to teach a nervous horse to cope with trail obstacles. It is wise to judge your own character before embarking upon such a training program. Otherwise, you may end up wasting your time and putting your horse through an unnecessary and unpleasant experience. A nervous person trying to train a nervous horse is like the proverbial "blind leading the blind."

The obstacle training for a nervous horse will be the same as that for a calm horse, except that you'll have to spend more time introducing your horse to each obstacle you wish to train him for. Once the horse has become sufficiently acquainted with each trail obstacle and begins to overcome his fears, his training will follow the same course as that of a normally natured horse.

The horse with a skittish nature will have a lot to cope with in the obstacle performance part of a western trail class, since many of the obstacles are designed just to test your horse's courage. These obstacles are enough to make a calm horse cautious about nearing them, so of course they can send a skittish horse into a frenzy.

One of the most common obstacles designed to test a horse's courage is plain water. Even some of the calmest and most tractable trail horses refuse to step in water for one reason or another, and a skittish horse may take quite some time to train for the water obstacle.

In trail classes featuring this obstacle, the water will either be a puddle on the ground or a tub of water large enough for your horse to take a few steps through. Horses who have not been trained for this obstacle almost invariably refuse to set foot in the water: this is a natural reaction.

Since water frightens most horses, it makes a good trail obstacle. Water offers a quick way to eliminate several horses from the competition in any trail class, so you will have to train your horse for water if you want to be pinned in this class.

While some of the trail obstacles are rather far-fetched in relation to their common occurrence on the trail, water does not fall into this category. It is a very reasonable obstacle in a trail class since you will often encounter water on the trail.

Sometimes you will allow your horse to go around or to jump a brook which crosses the trail, but in other instances this would be dangerous or even impossible. It is important that your horse trust you enough to wade through water at your direction.

Water frightens horses for several reasons. The rushing noise of moving water can scare a horse, as can the sight of moving water. The reflection of his image in still water can also unnerve your horse. He has no way of knowing how deep the water is or whether it contains such harmful objects as snakes, so of course he may be hesitant to step in it.

If your horse has ever had a bad experience or has been injured in water, he may have a very deep-rooted fear of it. You cannot expect to dispel such a fear quickly. If this is the case, approach the task with understanding.

One way to help overcome your horse's fear is to dismount and lead him to the water obstacle instead of asking him to wade through it with you mounted. This is not permissible in the show ring during a trail class, but it is a good way to at least get started in your training for the water obstacle.

When your horse is within a few steps of the water, stop leading him. Stand still and let him sniff the water. Somehow you've got to convince him that the brook is exactly the same thing that he drinks from his water bucket, and is equally harmless. However, the horse doesn't see his water bucket when he looks at a stream or brook; he envisions a large body of water, threatening to engulf him.

If you show your horse that you are not afraid of the water, he may follow suit. Take a few steps into the water to show your horse that it is not too deep for him to step in. You may be able to coax him into the water this way, but be careful in doing so.

If you stand in the water and try to pull your horse toward you, he may try to leap the water and in the process land on your foot or knock you down. To be safe, always lead your horse into water by walking at his side.

Your horse may balk when you try to lead him this way, but at least he cannot hurt you. If he refuses to step near or into the water, don't try tugging on his bridle or lead rope. You're sure to be the loser in any tug-of-war contest with your horse, for he is far stronger than you are. Pulling on a nervous horse will only make him more excitable, so don't even attempt it or you may be defeating your own purpose.

If your horse totally refuses to set foot anywhere near the water during your first training session, don't extend the lesson too long. Try coaxing him into the water for a few minutes, but don't by any means go on for hours. An unpleasant training session will only serve to make your horse more obstinate toward water. Take things slowly.

Try to get your horse into the water each day during your pleasure ride. Day by day, he should get closer to the water. Once he sets one foot in the water, he is on his way to overcoming his fear. From then on, it will just take time.

One thing that may speed along the process of teaching your horse to wade through water is to have him step in every puddle you see in the road on your daily pleasure ride. After all, a puddle is the same thing as a stream—only smaller. Since you are starting his training step by step, a puddle makes a logical beginning.

You should not have to dismount to get your horse to walk through a shallow puddle. When you near the puddle, your horse may be in the habit of avoiding it completely. If you feel him starting to move around the puddle, turn his head in the direction of it. If somehow your horse manages to maneuver himself past the puddle without stepping in it, turn him around and make him step in the puddle. After that, he should be willing to step in succeeding puddles.

Once he is going through puddles with no major objection, you should be able to ride your horse through the brook you had been leading him through. When you try it mounted, be prepared for anything to happen. Horses are especially adept at pulling all kinds of tricks to keep from stepping in water. These include shying, backing up, rearing, bucking, turning and bolting off, or jumping—all of which can result in the rider being dumped into the water.

To avoid these things, you'll have to anticipate anything your horse might do at the water crossing. Since you know him and his fears better than anyone else, your horse should not be able to surprise you. Expect from him any action that is common to him in such situations.

As long as you can anticipate any type of refusal your horse may put up at the water obstacle, eventually you should be able to get him to cross the water without unseating you. Once he has crossed his first small stream, you should have no trouble getting your horse to repeat the action.

However, horses sometimes have a way of performing an obstacle well on a pleasure ride, but refusing it totally in the show ring. Your horse may wade through trail streams willingly, and then refuse to go anywhere near the water obstacle in the show ring.

If he does refuse to step in the water in the ring, that is something only time and practice can cure. Some judges will allow some schooling in the ring, so you may want to ask the judge if he'll allow you to make your horse go through the water, although you may have been disqualified from the class competition.

This is the best recourse to take after your horse has refused an obstacle in the ring, if the judge gives you his okay. Correct your horse promptly, but do not punish him verbally or with a slap. Turn him around instead and head him toward the obstacle again. If he refuses, dismount and walk him through the water.

Now your horse knows he cannot get away with refusing an obstacle he has already performed well on the trail. It is vital to correct him immediately. If he gets away with refusing once, your horse is sure to try it again and again, and you'll really have a problem on your hands. You must always correct him as soon as he behaves incorrectly.

When your horse finally resigns himself to the fact that you are the boss, he will become much easier to train. Since the water obstacle can be the most frightening of all to horses, this may require the longest time of all your training for trail class. You must stick with it and correct your horse every time.

Unlike other trail obstacles, passing through water does not require a specific skill. While the gate obstacle requires the mastery of three skills on the horse's part, the water obstacle requires only willingness and courage. For this reason, any horse can learn to do the water obstacle. As long as you make him go through the water every time, your horse will eventually give up his fight and submit to your wishes.

BRIDGES

Water is a formidable obstacle for many horses, and a bridge can be twice as frightening. Not only does the horse have to cope with the water he sees passing under the bridge, but he also has to get up enough courage to step across the bridge.

Horses have a great mistrust of bridges, and are very hesitant to walk over them. Some horses will go to any lengths to avoid stepping on a bridge, even to the point of preferring to wade through the waters below instead of passing over the bridge.

In the case of water, at least a horse knows what he is dealing with. Although the water may frighten the horse with its rushing sound, most horses will swim through water if they have to. Some even enjoy swimming.

However, when it comes to crossing a bridge, the horse does not know exactly what he may be facing. When he sets one hoof on the bridge, he may feel it move slightly under his weight. The horse knows he is a heavy animal, and will not voluntarily step on anything he is not certain can support his weight.

Horses may have little common sense in some areas, but their fear of bridges is justified. Any horse who has had his leg crash through a poorly constructed bridge is well aware of the dangers of stepping on such a structure. More likely than not, a horse who has had a bad experience like this will be deathly afraid of bridges.

Whether or not your horse has been injured on a bridge, he may still have a natural fear of crossing bridges. One reason why bridges are a common obstacle in trail classes at the

Crossing bridges requires special care and attention. These western trail horses are calm enough not to spook on this small bridge which goes over railroad tracks. If your horse is not this calm, your best bet is to dismount and lead him over the bridge.

larger horse shows is that they offer a good test of a horse's courage. Since many horses are afraid of bridges, this obstacle eliminates many riders from the competition.

Another reason for this obstacle, of course, is that bridges are often found on trail rides. Although trail horses can wade through or jump small streams, there are some waters you will encounter on the trail that are just too much for a horse to handle.

Bridges are constructed over trail waters which may be too deep or rapid for a horse to wade through safely. Other dangers in the water may include sharp rocks or poisonous snakes. In these cases, a bridge is an absolute necessity. Unless your horse will walk over the bridge, you'll have to turn around and ride home.

Your horse may accept some bridges but not others. Bridges come in a wide variety of types, from the most primitive to the most modern constructions. Your horse may not believe a crude bridge is strong enough to support him, while a large modern bridge may intimidate him by its size alone. Bridges you may come across on a pleasure ride or trail ride range from a wide board stretched across the banks of a narrow stream to a huge suspension bridge spanning a wide river. The large bridge has an additional factor that may frighten your horse—traffic.

The way you cross a traffic bridge will be different than the way you cross a simple wooden bridge. If there is any way to avoid crossing a large bridge, do so. Bridges are dangerous enough in themselves, and are doubly so when the element of traffic is added.

Many large bridges have a walkway for use by pedestrians and bicyclists. Don't by any means think you'll be safer in walking your horse out there. The walkway eliminates the traffic problem, but it creates another one.

From the walkway, your horse can look over a short railing and see the deep waters below him. The sound of the traffic on his other side may cause your horse to lean toward the railing. When he realizes there is danger on both sides of him, your horse may go into a total panic. In some horrible cases, horses have been so panic-stricken that they have bolted over the bridge railing.

Although traffic can be dangerous, you are better off coping with it than in risking the dangers of the walkway. Speed limits on bridges are considerably slower than on roads, so at least the traffic should be moving at a reasonably safe speed.

When crossing a large bridge, always dismount and lead your horse across as a precaution. Be alert to the traffic around you. If a car approaches rapidly enough from the rear to scare your horse, signal the driver to slow down.

This advice also holds for crossing a highway bridge. Although such an overpass goes above a highway instead of water, it can be just as frightening to your horse. The moving traffic below can bewilder your horse even more than water might. Be sure to observe traffic signs. Horses are not allowed on some highways, overpasses, and bridges.

Actually, you do not need to worry much over whether your horse will walk over a large bridge, for he will never be asked to negotiate anything like that in a trail class. If your horse will go over a large bridge, however, he should have little or no trouble with a small one.

A bridge in a trail class is usually a simple affair. It may be a wide and heavy board lifted a few inches above a puddle, or it may be a bit more sophisticated. In any case, the bridge will be a wooden structure over shallow water, much like you would find on the trail.

At smaller shows, the trail class obstacles are sometimes not as true-to-life. The "bridge" at such a show may be just a large piece of wood or tarpaper lying flat on the ground.

Some horses may step across this imitation bridge with no hesitation, since there is no water around and since the structure is not lifted off the ground. However, other horses who have been trained for a real bridge may have trouble adjusting to an imitation bridge. The horse does not realize that the piece of tarpaper is supposed to represent a bridge. To him, the tarpaper is a foreign object on the ground and he sees no reason why he should step across it when he can see plenty of free space on every side.

Given his choice, most any horse would walk around this "bridge." In western trail classes the judge expects the horse to obey the rider, so you must direct your horse to step on the bridge instead of walking around it.

As your horse advances toward the obstacle, you may have to urge him on gently with your legs. When a horse spies the tarpaper ahead, he will sometimes slow down or even come to a dead stop. In order to avoid this, give your horse a little encouragement with leg pressure before he thinks about hesitating.

As he draws closer to the bridge, your horse may try to head off in another direction. Usually a horse who intends to avoid the obstacle will head straight toward it and then veer off suddenly to the side when he gets closer than he wants to be to the "bridge."

If your horse starts to head off to the left of the obstacle, turn his head toward the right and apply pressure with your left leg. This will get him heading back in the direction of the bridge, in a straight line toward it.

Although you have corrected your horse and set him back on the proper course, he may still stray before you reach the obstacle. If he headed off toward the left at first, he may now try to veer off toward the right. Be careful not to apply too much pressure in turning him, or your horse will "oversteer" and turn too far in the opposite direction.

When a horse starts heading away from the bridge far enough back from it, you may end up correcting him in a series of his attempts to walk away from the obstacle. He'll head to the left and you will correct him; then he'll head to the right and you will correct him again.

To an onlooker straight ahead, this will make it look like your horse is wobbling back and forth sideways, almost in the manner of a drunken person. To the judge, it will be obvious that you are struggling to keep your horse heading toward the bridge. This will surely count against you, for a good trail horse should not put up such resistance to any trail obstacle.

However, in all fairness, a horse does have a right to be wary of a tarpaper "bridge." The wind may send the paper flying, which is enough to startle any horse. Your horse may prefer to step on a solid bridge anchored to the ground rather than a flimsy tarpaper imitation.

However, he has no choice in the show ring. You must prepare your horse in advance for any obstacle he may encounter in the trail class, whether it is real or imagined. You have no way of knowing which obstacles will be in a coming trail class, so the wisest thing is to be prepared for anything.

The only way to prepare your horse for the tarpaper bridge is to have him step on paper bags and other such objects you may come across on your daily pleasure rides. If you have a large sheet of plastic or a wide wooden platform handy, put it on the ground and ride your horse over it.

You may have to coax him over the object the first time by dismounting and leading him over it. The rustling sound of the plastic as he steps on it may make your horse nervous, but he should settle down after he has walked over it a few times.

After the first time, don't lead your horse anymore. Insist that he walk over the "bridge" with you mounted, or he may begin to use this as a trick to get you off his back at every obstacle he meets.

Horses are quick to pick up bad tricks like this, and slow to "un-learn" them. Once your horse has learned a way to make you dismount, he will use it again and again, as long as you continue to let him get away with it, and it's better to keep him from forming such bad habits in the first place.

STRANGE ANIMALS

Although the horse is a large animal, he may have a great fear of other animals which are smaller than he is. A test of a horse's courage with other animals is sometimes used in trail classes.

The animal used is usually a small one which you may meet on the trail, such as a racoon. Larger animals like dogs are never used as a test in a trail class, since the horse has every right to be afraid of a dog which might chase him and nip at his heels.

The animal used for the test will surely be a gentle one.

Sometimes a pet of the stable which is holding the show is used, so the animal will be used to horses. However, that does not necessarily mean your horse may be used to that type of animal.

A small, gentle animal cannot badger the horse the way a dog can, but the horse may still want nothing to do with it. This can cause you to lose points in a trail class if one of the tests is based on your horse's reaction to a small animal.

The animal is kept in a wire cage at one point in the show ring. Since the obstacles are set up in a series around the edge of the ring, you will go along to each obstacle you meet as you circle the ring. However, when your horse sees this obstacle ahead, he may have second thoughts about going any closer.

The sight of the wire cage in itself is enough to make some horses nervous, and when the horse sees the moving animal inside the cage he may decide not to take one step further.

If your horse does balk, you can dismount and lead him to the cage. It is better if your horse will walk all the way up to the cage before he stops, but don't fight him if he won't. It looks better to the judge if you lead your horse calmly to the obstacle, instead of remaining mounted and having to kick to get him to move.

As soon as you feel your horse begin to tense up when nearing the cage, stop him and dismount immediately. If you wait too long or try to make him take a few more steps, the horse may begin to edge away from the cage. He may even turn and try to bolt in the opposite direction. The minute the judge notices the slightest bit of hesitation in your horse, he will mark you down in points.

You have to be aware of your horse's every motion. If you remain alert, you will sense your horse's hesitation coming even before he slows down or stops. Keep in tune with your horse's body movements and muscle reflexes, and this will enable you to anticipate his next action.

If you are alert, your horse will sense it. This may even discourage him from trying to pull any tricks, such as walking past the obstacle. If your horse realizes that you are alert to his actions, he may not even bother to try to out-think you. In any case, you can get one step ahead of the game by staying alert.

This should enable you to anticipate when your horse is going to stop before the cage obstacle. He may even set a pattern of stopping a certain distance from it each time. If so, you should be able to guess just about where your horse will stop. Knowing this is good, but being able to keep him walking all the way up to the cage is better. The latter is really what the judge expects of you.

If your horse will approach the cage, don't dismount until you are as close to it as possible. Then dismount slowly, making sure your horse is facing the cage. Since your horse may be afraid of the moving animal in the cage, you must be honest with him at all times. Don't try to trick him into approaching the cage at an angle where he cannot see the animal. You'll only end up defeating your own purpose, for the horse will probably be startled when he does notice the animal. At that point, he may shy, rear, or even bolt away.

Instead, if you lead the horse confidently straight toward the animal cage, he will already be prepared by the time he reaches the obstacle. The horse will not react so violently, because seeing the animal will not be such a shock. The horse may still be a bit apprehensive, but he will be nowhere near as taken by surprise as he would be if you had tricked him into approaching a seemingly empty cage.

When you are close enough to reach the cage with your hand after you have dismounted, open the latch slowly. Pull the door open and lift the animal out. The most common way to do this is to use one hand to pick up the animal, while holding the reins in your other hand. However, it is possible to use both hands to pick up the animal if your reins are knotted together at the ends. That way, you can slip the reins over one arm, freeing both hands to open the cage and lift the animal out.

Using one or two hands on the animal is a matter of personal preference, but it may be safer to keep one hand on the reins in case your horse becomes excited. This will give you more control over him.

Whether you use one or two hands to handle the animal, be sure to hold onto the reins somehow. If your horse is calm, you may be tempted to show off this good trait by not holding the reins at all. No matter how gentle your horse is, something other than the animal may suddenly frighten him. If you aren't holding onto the reins, your horse may bolt away.

This will not impress the judge in your favor, to say the least. If your horse does run off, the judge will mark you down severely, maybe even to the point of disqualification. If you are lucky and your horse stands by calmly as you lift out the animal, the judge may still mark you down for your poor judgment for not taking the precaution of holding onto the reins.

Remember, you are being judged just as your horse is. Although it is the horse's performance that counts in a trail class, the judge also watches the rider closely. Good performance by a horse should be the result of good instruction to the horse from the rider. Always think before you act in the show ring, keeping in mind what the judge expects of you and your horse.

Since your horse should remain calm at each obstacle, you can help ensure this by acting in a calm manner. Move slowly and confidently, being careful not to let the cage door slam shut.

Show the animal to your horse first from a distance, as you lift it from the cage a few feet away from the horse's nose. Then move the animal slowly toward the horse. Stop a foot or two from the horse and let him stretch his neck out to sniff the animal.

Once the horse has satisfied his curiosity about the animal, you can mount, holding the animal. Grasp the reins and saddle horn in your left hand, while holding the animal in your right hand.

Swing gently up into the saddle, and set the animal in front of you on the seat. Pause a moment to show the judge that you have completed the test successfully. Then dismount the same way you mounted and return the animal to its cage.

Although mastery of this test is not as vital as some of the other trail skills, it can come in handy. You may find an injured animal on the trail and decide to give him a ride to your home or to the vet.

Handle the animal gently, whether you are on the trail or in the show ring. If it is wild or injured, the animal may bite you. Hold it behind the neck so it cannot reach far enough to bite.

You may want to practice this with a domestic animal at your home. If the animal is used to horses, you should have no problem. Be careful if you use a cat, for it may scratch the horse and frighten him about other small animals.

Even if you do practice at home, you cannot predict how your horse will react to an animal in the show ring. However, as long as you act calmly and stay alert to your horse's actions, you should be able to complete the animal obstacle successfully.

TIRES

Another common obstacle in a trail class is a group of tires. Your horse is expected to walk through the tires without tripping or becoming excited.

Western trail horses usually perform well at the tire obstacle, since they are sturdy animals and are used to rugged terrain. If you are competing in an open trail class, this will give you an advantage over the English entrants.

By their nature and training, English trail horses are generally more refined than their western counterparts. Accordingly, the English horse may be more timid and hesitant at the tires. Some English horses are totally confused by this rough obstacle. In contrast, Western horses often take to the tire obstacle with no hesitation. The horse may see the tires as something difficult to walk through, but he probably will not be as surprised at the sight of the tires as the English horse.

Since western horses are accustomed to rugged terrain and sticky footing situations, yours should have no trouble picking his way through the tire obstacle.

Although your horse may take naturally to the obstacle, there is always the chance that he may not. Your horse may require special training for the tire obstacle, however, if for some reason he objects to walking through it.

There are several reasons why some horses dislike this obstacle: some are frightened by the tires as foreign obstacles lying on the ground, while others may be afraid of getting their feet caught in the tires. Whatever your horse's fear, you'll have to help him overcome it if he is to compete successfully in trail classes.

The tire obstacle can be an amusing one for spectators at horse shows, since every horse has a different way of going through the tires. Some seem to take "one step forward and three backward" until they finally get through the series, while other horses almost run through the tires.

A calm horse will pick his way slowly through the tires. He may lower his head somewhat, to help keep himself in balance and to keep an eye on the tires. Give him a very slack rein in this event, for your horse needs leeway to make his way through the tires.

The horse actually performs this obstacle himself, with little help from the rider. Since the tires are arranged side by side and in rows (see illustration), you cannot steer your horse through them. The tires are closely packed so you will have to rely on your horse to pick his own path through them. His sense of balance and his natural surefootedness should be enough to guide your horse through the obstacle.

Although it is up to your horse to execute the main job here,

you can help make the job easier for him. Since the horse will have to concentrate on maintaining his balance, you should lift your weight from the horse's back slightly. Do this by pushing your weight into the stirrups. You may even stand in the stirrups somewhat, but don't exaggerate this by standing up completely.

Try to keep your weight evenly over the horse's back, or even lean slightly toward the front. Don't push your weight back, or you will be working against the forward movement of the horse, and this will make the task more difficult for him.

Sometimes the obstacle is not a laughing matter at all, for horses do injure themselves occasionally. A horse who tries to rear and bolt halfway through the series of tires may catch his feet and possibly break a leg. If your horse is terribly afraid of tires, don't even take him through them in the ring. Walk right past the tires. It is better to lose a few points than to lose your horse.

There are ways you can try to prepare your horse for the tires, however. If your horse is used to the sight of tires, you won't have much of a problem.

Tires can be used in training for several events. If you use them often, your horse should not have a great fear of tires in the show ring. You may even want to leave a tire lying in one end of your horse's corral. Then he will accept it as a part of his home, and he won't react with fear when he sees tires in the show ring.

Competition in the tire obstacle part of a trail class will make any rider appreciate a horse who is calm and not afraid. There is no way you can safely get a skittish horse through a series of tires. If you selected a trail horse with a gentle disposition, you will really appreciate this trait when your horse comes up against the tire obstacle in the show ring.

You can practice the tire obstacle at home if you have several tires to use. It is a good idea to ride your horse through the tires once every week or so, but do not overdo it. Walking through tires does not require a great amount of skill or training, so you should not spend too much time on it. Too much practice will only bore your horse, and may turn him against participating at the tire obstacle in the show ring.

OTHER OBSTACLES

While the gate, bridge, animals, and tires are the most common trail class obstacles, different shows may offer other tests for the trail horse.

The variety of these tests is limited only by the imagination of the people who organize the horse show. When you enter a trail class, you should be prepared to do anything.

While the judge will expect a good trail horse to be familiar with obstacles like the gate and bridge, he will also expect the horse to be able to adapt to any surprise obstacle.

Since the most important traits of a trail horse are his maneuverability and calmness in any situation, these surprise obstacles can offer the best tests of the western trail horse. Therefore, you must come to the trail class prepared for the standard obstacles, but you must also expect the unexpected.

5. Jumping

Aside from the trail class obstacles we have already covered, the only other task your horse will be asked to perform in the ring is jumping.

Although the western horse is not generally considered a jumper, many western trail horses do well at the jumps in trail classes. The western horse does not have the long and lanky legs required of a jumper, but he does have muscular hindquarters and enough spunk to get him up and over a small jump.

Your horse will not be asked to jump any higher than 18 inches in a western trail class. For a jump this low, little training is necessary. However, you will have to work with your horse enough to be sure he will take the jump willingly.

Much more training would be required if you were preparing your horse for high stadium jumping. Western horses are not allowed in such events, but at small shows they are allowed to enter open jumping classes where the jumps are never higher than 3 feet or 3 feet 6 inches.

It would be unfair to ask your horse to jump any higher in western tack. The western rig weighs about 20 pounds more than an English jumping saddle, and is not constructed for jumping. It is also impossible to sit in proper jumping position in a western saddle. Your weight will be further back than it should be, making the hard job of jumping even more difficult for your horse.

As a rider, it will even be more difficult for you to jump your horse when he is in western tack. You cannot grip with your knees as you would in an English saddle, and your legs will be extended too far. The only way you can make an adjustment is to stand up in your stirrups and lean forward as your horse goes over the jump which requires good balance on the part of the rider. When the horse lands, you will absorb the shock of impact in your feet. If you aren't balanced, you may lose your stirrups or even be jarred from the saddle.

After all, a western saddle was not designed for jumping. It is suitable for low jumps up to the 18-inch-high ones in trail class. If you are planning to jump higher than that, switch your horse to English tack or jump him bareback.

Sometimes it is best to start your horse's training for trail class jumping in English tack anyway. Since jumping takes a great amount of strength and muscular development, beginning the training with light gear makes it easier on your horse. Using an English bridle and reining with two hands may also make it easier to direct your horse over the jumps.

Use a snaffle bit if you are going to use English tack. This will prevent you from hurting the horse's mouth when he touches ground after the jump. A gentle western trail horse will go well in a snaffle, whereas an unruly one will not. Here is another phase of your trail horse's training which will be much easier if you were wise enough to choose a gentle horse.

If you did not pick a tractable horse, he may be quite uncontrollable in a snaffle. In that case, you'll have to use a stronger bit. This will make the whole training more difficult, for you will have to keep enough contact with the horse's mouth to keep him under control without hurting his mouth with the strong bit.

If your horse is so unruly that he fights every jump and tries to bolt away when you urge him into a lope preceding the jump, he is definitely not jumper material. Stick to low jumps with him in order to avoid injury to either of you.

You may want to take your horse to a professional trainer who can guarantee to break your horse of his bad habits in jumping, if you feel he is worth the expense of training. You will have to be trained as well, or your horse may not perform as well for you as he does for the professional trainer.

The only instance when such training is really worthwhile is in the case of a horse with true jumping potential which you cannot bring out yourself. Otherwise, train him yourself for low jumps and stick to trail classes instead of trying open jumping classes.

Since trail class jumps are so low, you won't have as much of a problem with the unruly horse in that class as you would in open jumping competition. There is no rule that says your horse must lope up to the jump in trail class. So if you keep him collected and ready to jump, you can have your horse approach the jump at any gait you wish.

Most horses do need to approach the jump at a lope, just to get up enough speed to propel their weight over the hurdle. The lope is a rhythmic gait which fits in well with a graceful jump. However, there are other ways of getting over a low jump.

You can trot your horse up to the jump if you feel that will give him enough impulsion to clear the obstacle. Many western trail class contestants favor this gait at the jump, for it can be easier to keep the horse from refusing the obstacle if he is at this more collected gait.

The jog is usually too slow for an approach to a jump. However, there are some horses who seem to take a jump from a standstill. They may approach the jump at a lope or a fast trot, but then they suddenly stop right before the jump. On a signal from the rider, the horse pops up over the jump. Horses who jump in this manner are the exception rather than the rule, and most need to build up some speed and maintain their forward motion all the way up to the jump.

Of course, there are some horses who refuse the jump in various ways: either they shy away from the obstacle, or they pass over it without jumping.

There are ways to get over an 18 inch hurdle without jumping, and your horse may be well aware of this. Some horses cannot be bothered to use the energy to jump such a low obstacle when they know they can just as easily walk over it.

Horses have different ways to get around jumping the hurdle. Some will rush toward it at full speed and then stop at the last minute. If you aren't prepared for this, the sudden jolt of stopping can send you flying.

Other horses may trot briskly toward the jump and continue to trot right over it. The trotting horse may also jump the obstacle with his front legs and trot over it with his hind legs.

Another horse may refuse to approach and take the jump at anything faster than a walk. This isn't exactly what the judge has in mind, but he'd rather see your horse go over the obstacle willingly at a walk than lope up to the jump and refuse it altogether.

Refusal of a jump can entail immediate disqualification. Most shows will allow you three tries, but others will not. In a trail class, you will be allowed to compete at the other obstacles, but the judge will mark you down if your horse refuses the jump.

If the trail class has many entrants and is taking longer than planned for, the jump may be used to narrow down the competition. The jump is often the first trail test you meet in the series of tests in trail class. In that case, if your horse refuses or knocks the jump down, you may be asked to leave the ring.

It is difficult to predict how your horse will react to a jump at any given try. If he senses the slightest nervousness in you, he may refuse because he knows you aren't ready for him to jump. Although you may be urging your horse to jump with your aids, your tense body tells the horse that you really do not want him to take the jump. So he won't.

Another thing that can make your horse refuse is the particular type of jump. In most trail classes, the jump is a simple one. Two posts on each side support a straight pole, which can be knocked off if the horse kicks it. This type of jump prevents any injury, for your horse cannot get caught in it.

If a different type of jump is used, your horse may be afraid of it. Jumps vary in trail classes. Some common ones are a bale of hay, a simple pole jump with brush in front of it, or a pole jump with a swinging sign hanging from it. The extra things like the brush and swinging sign can frighten your horse. If he has any qualms about jumping in the first place, these obstacles will surely dissuade him from taking this jump in class.

While this will be the case with many western trail horses, there are exceptional horses who have no fear of any jump. In fact, while training for low jumps you may find your horse does rather well at them. If you develop a taste for jumping in the process, you may want to go into additional jumper training with your horse, aside from what he will be asked to jump in a western trail class.

Although most western trail horses are basically not jumpers, some hold their own in competition against English hunters. If your horse has been taught to respond to English reining, there is no reason why you cannot train him as a hunter.

The idea that western horses can make fine hunters is proven by the fact that there is now such a label as the "Quarter Horse

Jumper." Since the traditionally western Quarter Horse has been recognized as a competent hunter in several cases, there is now no question that a western trail horse can be trained for the hunt course.

Many horses bred in the West and shipped to the East for sale are originally broken western, but are later trained to go English. A horse like this is versatile, and can be shown in many classes.

Your western trail horse may fall into this category. If you notice during your pleasure rides that your horse tends to jump a log in his path when he could just as easily walk over it, you may have the makings of an English hunter.

There are other signs which indicate a horse has a potential for jumping. Some horses are spotted as jumpers when they are still foals. The colt or filly who constantly tries to jump over the corral fence may later become a fine jumper.

When a horse changes hands from one owner to another, he is often trained for another style of riding. Sometimes a western rider owns a potential hunter, but never trains the horse to jump because he has no background in riding jumpers.

An English rider may come along and spot the horse's potential. After working with the horse for several months, the rider will have trained the horse as a fine hunter.

Just because you introduce a new form of riding to the horse doesn't mean he will forget his early western training. There is no reason why a horse cannot be ridden and shown both English and western. Many horses look fine and perform well in both types of tack, so you should not limit your horse's possibilities.

A horse who can be ridden both English and western, and who is trained to jump and perform at trail obstacles, will be very valuable indeed. He makes an excellent all around horse.

If you have knowledge of English jumping, you may train your horse yourself. If you have only ridden western (or English on the flat) you'll need to take jumping lessons from a qualified instructor. If you can persuade the instructor to give you lessons on your horse, both you and your mount can learn together.

Otherwise, you will have to bring home the skills you learn at your lessons and apply them to your horse. As you gain confidence and skill from your lessons, you will be able to take your own horse over jumps of increasing height.

The best way to start your horse's training is not with you on his back, approaching a 3-foot jump. Instead, take things from the beginning and advance slowly. That is the only way your horse can learn well.

If you do not have standard jumps to use for practice, you can substitute. Two cardboard boxes will do to support each side of the jump post if you invert them so that the open side is facing the ground. A long pole, or even a broom handle, can be laid across the two boxes to simulate a jump.

Put your horse in his halter with a lead rope attached. Stand to the left of his head, holding the lead rope just under his chin. Begin to walk toward the jump.

When you get in front of it, say "UP!" and have your horse walk over it. Don't worry if he knocks it down. That may well happen at the walk since he won't be moving fast enough to pick his feet up very high.

As long as your horse is not afraid of the jump, you can go on with his training. Approach the jump beside your horse, with him at a jog. Again give the command "UP!" and have your horse trot over the jump.

Then you can try it mounted, at the trot. When your horse nears the jump, stand in your stirrups, lean forward, and say "UP!" Your horse may jump this time, or may still trot over the jump.

After enough practice at the trot, you can work on getting your horse to take the jump from a lope. There is little chance of him trying to lope over the jump, so if you can get him to take the jump, he will probably jump it correctly.

Depending on your horse's progress, you can start increasing the height of the jump gradually. Be sure not to push your horse beyond his limit: a western-type Quarter Horse may have powerful hindquarters to propel him over the jump, but he also has short legs.

Although he may do well at jumps of medium height (between 3 and 4 feet), the Quarter Horse's physical limitations will keep him from competing in stadium jumping, where the fences go as high as 6 and 7 feet.

Jumping is a demanding task, and it can be dangerous if you do not compete in it wisely. If you push your horse to take a jump beyond his capabilities, he may very possibly injure himself and you in the process.

Hunt courses include a great variety of jumps, ranging from a simple bale of hay to the coop jump. The stiffer competitions include jumps up and downhill, over brush, and over water.

Unless your western trail horse is very exceptional or has been especially well-schooled at jumping, a hunt course like this will probably be too much for him to handle.

Don't press your luck: know your horse's limitations and work within them. The western trail horse is versatile, but only to a reasonable point. If you understand this from the beginning, you can train your horse to compete in events in which he will win you many ribbons.

6. *The Trail Class*

Now that you and your horse have mastered the basic skills and are working as a team, you are ready to begin competing in western trail classes in the show ring.

Although learning skills is vital for competition, skill is not all there is to a winning show ring performance. Along with mastery of skills, a certain showmanship is often required to impress the judge.

Showmanship entails many factors, such as preparation, grooming, appearance, and show ring manners. Executing the judge's commands largely determines your score in a class, but your general showmanship can have an effect on whether you place first or second.

When your performance and that of another rider are nearly tied, your showmanship may well be the deciding factor. Little things can influence the judge, so it is best to make everything you can work in your favor.

There are numerous ways to impress the judge, referred to as "show ring tactics." Some may work better on one judge than on another, but one basic rule of thumb will bring you luck with any judge—be serious about competition, but always remain a good sport.

Look at the judge as a person. He will certainly favor a rider who tries his hardest in the ring but never goes so far as to infringe on the rights of another contestant. On the other hand, a sour-faced rider who cuts others off and whips his horse will make a very bad impression on the judge. If you enter other classes in the same or other shows which are judged by the same man, he will remember your attitude and surely will not favor you at all.

While your score in a trail class is based on your horse's performance, the judge will also be sizing you up as a rider. A contestant who brings out a good performance in his horse by the proper methods will look better in the judge's eyes than will a rider who abuses his horse in the ring.

Many shows demand immediate disqualification of any rider who is cruel to his mount. This includes excessive use of crop or spurs, slapping the horse often on the neck or head, kicking him constantly, or verbal abuse.

Punishing your horse by the use of your voice may be effective in practice sessions at home, but it has no place whatsoever in the show ring. Just as the old adage about children goes, riders in the ring should be "seen but not heard."

The aids you may use in the show ring are your hands, arms, feet, legs, and body position. Verbal commands only serve to indicate that you cannot control your horse with the proper aids.

While speaking in the ring is not advisable, the worst thing you can do in the ring is to use foul language. This demonstrates several negative factors about you to the judge. It shows that you are impolite, frustrated with the horse you obviously cannot control, and a poor sport on top of it all.

You should be on your best behavior in the ring. If your horse disobeys, you may correct him—but do not punish him verbally or physically, for this will only lower you in the eyes of the judge.

When your horse does do something wrong in the ring, store the incident in the back of your mind. Later, at home, work on your horse's performance at the particular task to prevent him from making the same mistake again in the show ring.

However, before you practice the task, review the show ring incident in your mind. Was the mistake really your horse's fault, or did you fail to communicate with him? Your answer will tell you whether to work more on your horse's training or to practice your own way of applying the aids.

Consider this carefully, for your horse's error may well have been your own fault. When a horse does not perform well, it is due to the rider's inability to give the proper signals to the horse in nine cases out of ten.

"The horse is always right" is an old saying, and it has a ring of truth. A horse will usually do what you tell him to. If he acts improperly, it probably means you have accidentally asked him to do something else by your unconscious actions. A rider who does not transmit the correct signals only confuses his horse, and often the rider does not get the desired response from his mount.

For example, a rider who wants his horse to halt can pull back on the reins all he wants, but the horse may not stop unless the rider uses his other aids at the same time. If the rider leans forward instead of shifting his weight backward, his body is telling the horse to walk on.

In this case, the rider's hands are telling the horse to stop, while his body is telling the horse to continue walking. Needless to say, this totally confuses the horse. He may respond to one aid or the other, but he probably won't do what you want him to, and will continue walking until all your aids ask him to halt.

In order to bring the correct response from your horse, you

must synchronize your aids: make them all work together, and apply them at the same instant. If you do this and your horse doesn't respond properly, it means one of two things: either your horse is only green broken and hasn't been trained to respond to the aids, or he has been trained and is simply disobeying you.

You must be very sure to apply the correct aids in the show ring when every action counts. You will receive a better score if your horse immediately responds in the correct way when you apply the aids, instead of your having to correct him.

All this is part of your overall showmanship. You and your horse will give a much more polished performance if you communicate the right signals and he responds well. A performance like this will appear smooth and flowing, and will be sure to impress the judge.

If you apply the aids properly, it will look to the judge as though your horse is responding to the command of the ring announcer. The best riders apply their aids so smoothly that the judge can barely discern any movement. Showmanship like this is the ideal you should be aiming for. It means that you must work at perfecting your application of the aids just as much as you work at training your horse for specific trail class skills.

In addition, there are other considerations you should keep in mind concerning show ring showmanship. While you must be considerate of the horse, you must give the same consideration to the other riders in the class. This involves many little things, but they are all important.

One factor is your method of bringing an unruly horse into the ring. If your horse kicks, by all means tie a red ribbon on his tail. The judge may mark you down slightly for this sign that your trail horse has the bad trait of kicking, but it is better to give the other riders fair warning. The judge will mark you down more severely if you don't tie a ribbon on your horse's tail and he kicks another horse in the ring.

Just as a kicker is a menace in the ring unless you keep an eye on him, so is the horse who bites. You can avoid biting problems by keeping your horse from getting too close to another in the ring. There is no way to let other riders know your horse bites, so it is up to you to make sure he doesn't get the chance. If you allow your horse to get close enough to bite another in the class, the judge will mark you down on two counts—for not maintaining the proper spacing between horses, and for having a trail horse who bites. Since a trail horse is supposed to be gentle and well-mannered, biting lowers his worth.

Your own manners as a rider are important as well. If you are going to ride past another horse, let the rider know by saying the word "passing" as you get close behind him. Pass to the inside of the ring, fast enough to get by the other horse, but not so fast as to frighten him.

Even if your horse forgets his manners, you must always maintain yours in the ring. Some horses are so excited in the ring that they bolt when given the command to lope. If your horse does go charging around the ring, ride him directly to the out gate and leave the ring before he causes an accident.

The judge will appreciate this exhibition of your consideration for your fellow riders. Since you have impressed him with your good judgment and manners this way, the judge will tend to look upon you with favor if you enter another class at the show.

One extra thing you can do to impress the judge is to ride with a smile on your face. This shows that you are relaxed and in control of your horse. A smile also shows that your horse is giving you a pleasant ride, which can help your score on the railwork part of the trail class.

While you are riding along the rail, be sure your horse does not cut corners. Horses can be lazy, and often tend to stray away from the rail and toward the center of the ring; this way, they do not have to go as far. A good rider should keep his horse close to the rail at all times, except when passing.

These photos by the author illustrate the proper western seat for show ring performance. The rider is Donna Stevens, a riding instructor at Green Acres Stables, Dover, New Hampshire. She is mounted on Grey Ghost, her horse. Actually Donna rides an English balance seat and hunt seat, and Ghost is a cross-country horse, but both adapt well to western riding.

Front view shows horse alert and standing square, with the rider's free hand on her thigh.

Back view shows horse standing almost square, except for his right rear leg, which is a bit too far forward. The rider would be sitting properly if the horse were standing exactly square—but since the horse's balance is slightly off, the rider's seat has shifted slightly to the left.

Upper portion of rider's body is straight and tall, with the hand held correctly just over the horse's withers. Since she is not using a pommel, the rider is holding the reins through one finger in her left hand.

Lower portion of rider's body shows the knee bent properly, with her heel down and the ball of the foot in the stirrup.

Total side view of rider shows all facets of the proper western seat. A straight line can be drawn from her head, to elbow, to heel.

With the horse in motion, the rider's seat stays the same. Here, her seat has shifted a bit too far forward by accident.

With the horse at a standstill, the seat is illustrated even better Again, the horse is not standing quite perfectly square.

Try not to pay attention to spectators on the rail. Nothing is worse than the "stage mother" who shouts instructions to the rider in the ring. If anyone does speak to you while you're in the ring, look straight ahead and pretend you don't hear them.

You must conduct yourself in a responsible manner in the show ring. Be alert, be courteous, be what the judge wants every rider to be—a thinking rider who does his job well.

APPEARANCE

The physical appearance of the horse and rider can have as great an influence on the judge as showmanship can. How you look reflects how you feel, and this can be an important consideration for the judge.

We are always told to dress well when meeting someone or applying for a job because it is said that "first impressions are lasting impressions." Although a person's worth is more important than his appearance, the first impression a stranger has of us is based on how we look. He sees us before we can speak, so his initial judgment is based on our appearance.

This is also true of the horse show judge. Before you get a chance to exhibit your horse's ability in a trail class, the judge will look you and your horse over as you walk into the ring. If you make a good impression on the basis of your appearance, the judge will naturally tend to keep a closer eye on you during the class.

This is only natural, because anyone likes to look at someone with a pleasant appearance. Our eyes are drawn to that which interests us. Certainly we would rather look at something pleasant than something unpleasant. The better you look, and the more striking your horse looks and acts, the more attention you will get from the judge.

Of course, there are cases when a horse with poor conformation gives such an outstanding ring performance that the judge has no choice but to give him top honors in the class.

However, unless you are an exception like this, a poor appearance will give the judge a bad impression.

After all, a horse show is just what the name says—a show. If you want to show something off, it is invariably something which looks nice and which will impress others with its beauty. You should make every effort to look your best at a horse show, and you should also be sure your horse is looking his best. You are a team, and must always think of yourselves as such.

A sloppy appearance tells the judge you really do not care about the show. A neat rider on an ungroomed horse indicates that you do not care for your horse; a sloppy rider on a groomed horse shows that the rider is a messy person.

You must dress in a way that shows you respect yourself, and you must groom your horse in a way that shows you care about him. Otherwise, the judge will look at you as an insult to the show. He will think you are either too lazy to fix yourself up for such an event, or that you are so inexperienced at showing that you don't even know the basic rule about looking presentable.

In a showmanship halter class, looks are all-important. This is not so in the trail class where your horse's performance is more important. However, when it comes down to choosing between two equally well performing horses, the judge is sure to pick the one who presents the best appearance.

This is only common sense. If you think about what you are trying to do in a horse show, it becomes obvious that you are trying to be chosen as the best. Anyone who is tops in his field never appears in public looking anything but his best. Old clothes are fine for your stablework and training sessions at home, but for the show ring you should wear the best you have.

This does not necessarily mean that you must wear an expensive riding outfit to the show. You will not impress the judge by wearing expensive clothing, but rather by dressing properly for the class.

Lining up in the show ring for the judging, these riders show a variety of good and poor ring techniques. The rider in the immediate foreground is sitting properly for the judge, but her horse is not standing square and is not alert. The rider in the middle of the line (wearing sunglasses) incorrectly has two hands on the reins and is looking at the camera, instead of where she should be looking—straight ahead. Her clothing is more showman-like than that of the rider in the foreground, but this inattentive rider will probably score lower when the judge observes her because of her actions. (Photo courtesy the American Quarter Horse Assn.)

Western clothing is generally practical and rugged, since it is designed for use out on the range. Although you should dress up a bit more for the show ring, don't overdo it. Dress sensibly and neatly, for that is all the judge expects of you.

The rider's attire in a western trail class can range from simple clean blue jeans and a western shirt to a complete western suit with matching jacket and pants. Any clothing is acceptable, as long as it is clean and proper for western riding.

Unless you are going to be showing a very flashy western horse, there is really no need to buy an expensive western suit. Take your horse's appearance into consideration when you choose your outfit, since you don't want to outshine him. Try to dress according to his looks.

Endurance trail riding competition demands a lot from a horse, and this is one who can take the demands and perform well. He is a registered Arabian gelding Prince Pancake, owned by Cliff Lewis of Reno, Nevada. While not a show horse, Prince Pancake is listed as a Top Endurance Trail Ride horse who competes in 50-mile-a-day and 100-mile-a-day events. (Photo courtesy the International Arabian Horse Assn.)

However, there are some standards for western attire in a show. To really look proper, you should wear an outfit at least as good as the following: western "cowboy" boots, bell-bottom or straight-leg pants in a solid color, a plain or printed western shirt, a wide leather belt with a silver western-style buckle, a bow tie or a bolo tie, and a western hat. If you want to wear a vest or chaps they will add nice extra touches to your outfit.

While clothing is a basic part of your appearance, another factor in your personal grooming for the show ring is your hair. A woman should be sure her hair is clean and styled neatly. If her hair is long, braids or ponytails are neat and add to the overall western look. However the hair is styled, it must be in a way that prevents it from flying in the rider's face. A woman's hair must not reach so far down the rider's back that it covers the show entry number which is pinned to her back.

Just as you must take pains to be sure your own grooming is done well, you must do the same for your horse. After all, he is really the one competing in a trail class. You are just up there to give him directions and as a complementary accessory. You should spend even more time on your horse's grooming for the show than you do on your own.

GROOMING YOUR HORSE

If you have been taking care of your horse properly every day, you will not have a big job in grooming him for the show ring. If you have not done this, you will have to begin preparing him through proper grooming several weeks ahead of the show date.

In the parts of the country which have cold winters, horse shows begin each spring around April or May. If you have not been grooming your horse well during the winter months, he probably has a thick winter coat. Had you brushed him daily he would have shed the coat gradually, but now you have a real chore ahead of you. A horse with a winter coat looks terrible in the show ring. The winter coat is much longer than the normal coat, and it hangs down in long strands or in clumps from the horse's back and sides. You will have to go to work on your horse with a shedding blade. Daily grooming and extensive use of the shedding blade should eliminate the winter coat in several weeks, if you really work at it.

If your horse still has a winter coat from your lack of daily grooming, chances are that his coat has lost its luster and shine. Just like human hair, a horse's coat must be brushed daily to help the oils from the skin circulate into the hairs. A horse who does not receive frequent brushing usually has a dull coat with flakes of white in it. This is just like human dandruff, and is caused by letting the skin dry out from not circulating its natural oils.

Another cause of a dull coat is improper feeding. Your horse should be fed a flake or two of hay plus two feedings of grain daily. You should provide him with a salt lick and keep water nearby. Proper feeding will keep your horse healthy and in good shape. If he does not feel good, he cannot look good.

If you have bought an underfed horse in the hopes of "fattening him up," be careful how you do this. Give him an extra quart of grain a day until he puts on weight, but don't stuff him with hay. Nothing looks worse than a horse whose ribs show, but who has a huge hay belly.

Do not show your horse until he is at the proper weight and condition. When you are feeding him well, grooming him daily, and exercising him often, he will begin to look good. After he has a good appearance, you must continue to take care of him this way. A judge is quick to spot a horse who does not receive the best of care.

Providing that your horse has been properly cared for and is in good shape, all you will need to do to ready him for a show will be to add the finishing touches.

Much of your work will be done the day before the show. If you want to do any last-minute practicing, do it in the morning. It will take you all afternoon to groom your horse properly, and you should let him rest all evening before the show the next day.

If you plan to show in a halter class, you may want to give your horse a bath. Don't do this before every show if you show often, or you will dry the horse's coat out. Once or twice a month is plenty, so don't bathe your horse more often than that.

You must take certain precautions if you are going to give your horse a bath. The weather can be an important factor, so think before you begin wetting your horse down. If it is a chilly day, your horse may well catch a bad cold; if it is a hot day, the shock of cold water can give him a heart attack.

As long as the weather is mild, it is safe to bathe your horse. If he is not afraid of hoses, the best way is to use a hose with an attachment that makes the water come out separated, as in a shower stall. This will wet him down quickly. You want to get the job over with as soon as you can, so you can get your horse dry again.

If you can rig up some outdoor crossties, they will make it easier to bathe your horse. If that is not possible, be sure he is either tied to something secure or held on a lead rope by a friend—otherwise, he is sure to run when you spray the water on him.

While you are wetting him with the hose, you should already have a bucket full of warm, soapy water nearby. With a sponge, you will apply the soapy water on your horse's back, and rub it in. Some horse owners prefer to use a tube of shampoo when bathing their horses, for it will make the coat very soft and shiny. If you do this, use a shampoo that adds oils or it may dry your horse's coat out too much.

Sometimes it is easier to soap the horse all over his body and then wash him off, but some horse owners prefer to wash one part of the horse at a time and then rinse each section. Whatever works best for you is fine.

When preparing for a halter showmanship class, some riders use a creme rinse on their horse's manes after they have rinsed the shampoo out. If you do this, you'll be surprised at how soft and fine your horse's mane and tail will feel. This is fine for a halter class, but for trail it really isn't necessary.

If for some reason your horse is deathly afraid of being bathed, don't push it on him all at once. Let him sniff the hose and the bucket. If he raises a big fuss every time, you may be just as well off to not bathe him at all. It isn't that important.

You should groom your horse with a curry comb and a soft brush both before and after the bath. If you have a rubber curry comb, you can use this while soaping the horse since it will clean him well.

After you have bathed your horse and washed the soap off, rub him all over with an old towel. Let his coat stay ruffled up, so the air can get in and dry it quicker.

Do not blanket your horse immediately after the bath, as this is one of the surest ways to give him a cold or even pneumonia. Walk him in big circles on a lead rope out in the air instead. It should only take about 15 to 20 minutes for your horse to dry off if it is a warm day.

After your horse is quite dry, you should groom him again and blanket him. Put him in a stall with clean bedding to keep him from getting dirty again. Let your horse rest for a while before you return to do the rest of the grooming.

Now that he is clean, you should work on particular bits of grooming to make him look his best in the ring. Trim all whiskers away from his nose, and cut them off as close as you can without snipping him. The same goes for the hair in his ears. In hot weather, trim the ear hair only so that it does not extend out of the ear. Your horse will need some hair to protect his inner ear from fly bites.

You should also trim any clumps of excess hair from your horse's fetlocks. They will look best if you have a set of electric clippers, but if not, do your best with scissors.

If his tail is ragged-looking, trim it off evenly at the end. Western horses do not need to have long flowing tails. Many have very short ones, especially Quarter Horses who are clipped.

The same goes for trimming your horse's mane. It should be even at the ends. If he wears it long, the mane should be long enough to lie flat on his neck. If his mane is clipped off western style, be sure it has not grown out too long. You may need to shave his mane off again.

This is all the preparation you will have to do the day before the show—but there will be more to do the next morning.

Certainly you will have to groom your horse thoroughly again the morning of the show. You may have to wash his legs with soapy water if he soiled them in his stall overnight. This is especially important if your horse has white stockings.

One other thing you can do to make your horse look even better is to apply shoe polish to his hoofs. Use black polish if your horse has black hoofs. Use clear polish for an Appaloosa-type horse with striped hoofs.

Needless to say, your horse's feet should be in proper repair long before the show date. He should either have properly fitting shoes, or should have trimmed barefoot hoofs. Whether or not you have him shod depends on the type of terrain you ride on most often. Shoes are vital for constant riding on paved streets, but are not necessary for horses who are ridden only on turf.

Just as your horse must be clean and in good shape, so must your tack. You should clean it thoroughly after your last ride before the show, whether that is the day before the show or earlier.

Thorough cleaning means taking the bridle completely apart and cleaning each section separately. If you don't have a special tack cleaner, you can use warm soapy water as long as you dry the tack immediately. The bit and silver pieces on the bridle should be cleaned with a steel wool pad to make them shine. You must also clean the saddle.

There are sprays made to clean tack, and there are also some made to spray on a horse's coat just before a show to make it take on a pretty sheen. It is up to you whether or not you want to use any of these products. Just do your best to make your horse look nice.

GETTING TO THE SHOW

Your task of grooming before the show will be different if you ride your horse to the show, ship him there in the morning, or keep him in a stall on the grounds the night before.

If the show is close enough and you ride to it, be sure to leave early enough. You should arrive at the show grounds an hour before the start of the first class so you will have time to register for classes and groom your horse again. He'll also need some time to rest from the ride there.

Your horse will probably get his feet or legs dirty again during the ride to the show. Bring grooming tools to the show with you so you can clean him up again before your first class.

If you have a friend who is willing to drive to the show and spend the day there, you will be better off. A friend with a pickup truck can bring hay, a water bucket, a blanket, and any other equipment you may need during the course of the day.

If you have a horse trailer or can rent one, you can bring your equipment along with you on the ride there. It is to your advantage to use a van and ship your horse to the show grounds, for he will stay cleaner and will not to be tired from a ride there. You will be able to tie your horse to the van or even put him in it between classes if the flies or weather are bad. You can also display your ribbons on the van.

Of course, the ideal situation would be to have a stall on the show grounds, and bring your horse to it the night before in a van. That way, your horse will already be accustomed to the show grounds and will have a place to rest between events.

Stalls are usually available for rent at shows which last more than one day. Smaller horse shows which are held at a local stable may have stalls available for only a few dollars if you want to keep your horse there the night before and the day of the show. If you can do this, it is a wise idea.

When you arrive at the show grounds that day, whether you ride, drive, or keep your horse there overnight, get a class list if you don't have one already. Choose your classes and sign up for them.

About ten minutes before your first class is scheduled to begin, tack your horse up and ride him around in the practice field. This should loosen him up, and he will be ready to compete in the class.

Always be on time for the class. The judge will not enjoy waiting for an entrant who is still tacking his horse up when the ring call is given to enter.

When you enter the ring for a western trail class, you will be asked to walk your horse along the rail until all the entrants are in the show ring. Then the class will begin competition.

What you will be asked to do next depends on the size of the show and on the particular judge. In most shows, trail class entrants first go through the various gaits along the rail. This will include several changes of gait and direction.

This is the pleasure part of the trail class, and it counts 30 percent in the judging. Your horse will be scored on how smooth a ride he appears to give, how quickly he responds to aids for a change of gait, and whether he takes the correct lead when told to lope.

When the railwork has been completed, the judge may ask all the entrants to line up in the center of the ring. At that time, the judge will examine each horse closely. In most trail classes, conformation counts for 10 percent of the judging. This is what the judge will be determining when the riders are lined up.

The judge may also try to lift your horse's hoof to see if he gives it willingly. He will notice whether the horse is standing square and is alert. The judge may ask you to dismount and mount again, to see if your horse will stand while you do this.

If there are many entrants in the class, the judge may not go into such detail. While the railwork and obstacles are mandatory, close examination of each mount is not. However, most judges do this to give everyone a fair chance, since it gives them a better idea of how good each horse would be on the trail.

While the judge is examining each horse in line, the ring attendants may be bringing in the obstacles and setting them up. Since the judge will have a few minutes to spend looking over the horses while that is being done, he may ask you a question or two when he comes to you in the line.

Answer his questions politely and honestly, but don't volunteer any information. The judge will ask you whatever he wants to know, and will not appreciate your telling him anything else. Just be cooperative.

When the judge has finished looking over each trail horse, the entrants will be asked to leave the ring until all the obstacles are ready. Then the contestants will be called into the ring one at a time to compete at the obstacle course.

This is where the main emphasis of the class lies, as the trail obstacles count for 60 percent of the judging. This stands to reason, since the best test of a trail horse is how well he can perform at common obstacles found on the trail.

The obstacles will probably be set up around the rail of the ring. You will start at the first one, and continue along the edge of the ring until you reach the next one. If your horse puts up too much of a fuss at one obstacle, the ring attendant may instruct you to pass it and go on to the next obstacle. Do as he says, for he is under instructions from the judge.

When all the riders have completed the obstacle course, they wait outside the ring until the winners are announced. If the judge calls your number, ride into the ring smiling, thank the judge for the prize, and take it proudly. You have earned it.

7. The Trail Ride

The trail ride is the total test of the western trail horse. It is the practical application of all the skills you have taught your horse for show ring performance in trail classes. While the trail class serves to exhibit your horse's ability to perform various trail skills, the trail ride depends on your horse's ability to apply these skills to a real trail situation.

This makes sense for, after all, what good is a skill unless it is put to use? An unused skill is just the knowledge of how to perform the task, but skill in use shows the worth of the task. Using the skill helps to develop and perfect it, and this is what you should be aiming at for trail competition.

The application of skills determines whether you win or lose, especially in a competitive sport like western trail riding. In a sport like this, the winners are those who practice their skills constantly.

In any competition, you want to give yourself as many breaks as possible. By keeping the skills you and your horse have in top condition, you give yourself one advantage over less ambitious entrants in the trail ride. If you're out there to win (and you should be), you owe it to yourself to enter the trail ride well prepared and in good condition for the event.

Too many riders enter trail rides fully unprepared. Most consider themselves ready to enter a competitive trail ride just because they occasionally ride their horses on trails for pleasure. These riders are the first to be knocked out of the competition, as soon as they realize how rigorous a trail ride can be. After a few hours on a competitive trail ride, these riders discover that competitive trail riding is one of the most demanding types of riding for both horse and rider.

For that reason, there is a great amount of preparation required for good performance on a trail ride. Before you can go into specific trail training, you must be sure you and your horse are both in excellent physical condition. A trail ride is a demanding physical experience for the horse, and requires him to exert himself more than he normally does.

Your job as rider is to complete the trail ride quickly enough to meet the time limit, but slowly enough to keep your horse from over-exerting himself: you must use your head to decide the timing while your horse uses his body to meet the plan you have set up.

Preparation for this activity depends on the type of trail ride you'll be competing in. A one-day affair obviously won't take as much preparation as a three-day trail ride, so you'll have to adjust your training to the specific trail ride.

Depending on the organization sponsoring the ride, it can vary from 10 to 300 miles. A 10-mile ride might be sponsored by a small group, such as 4-H, for its members only. More common is a 40-mile trail ride, which takes one full day and is usually sponsored by a small- or medium-sized riding club.

A larger riding club might offer a 100-mile trail ride, lasting three days. Similar to this is the statewide trail ride, offered in several small states.

The 300-mile trail rides are rather uncommon nowadays, since civilization has limited open riding spaces. A ride this long is usually found only out West, where there are still some open prairies for long stretches of riding.

The difference in preparing for and competing in these trail rides is vast. Little preparation is required for a 10-mile ride, since a horse in good condition should be used to this amount of riding nearly every day. However, only horses and riders in top condition should enter the 300-mile ride.

Since these two extremes are not as common as the 40-mile, 100-mile, and statewide trail rides, we will not go into depth on preparing for them. Instead, it is best to concentrate on the more common trail ride lengths, since these are what most trail competitors will be dealing with.

The type of training you'll be doing depends largely on the terrain you'll be covering on the trail ride. If it is the type of terrain your horse is accustomed to, you won't have to worry too much about it. If it is rougher than you usually ride on, you'll have to condition your horse to it before you go on the trail ride.

The main type of terrain that will require conditioning in your horse is land which is hilly or rocky. Horses who are used to being ridden on flat plains will have a hard time coping with a hilly path on a trail ride. Since trail rides are constructed to test your horse's endurance, you can expect a good deal of rough terrain on any competitive trail ride.

If you generally ride your horse daily for pleasure, as do most riders, you probably don't choose rugged terrain for your riding. For this reason, you may have to do quite a bit of conditioning to ready your horse for a trail ride, especially if it is one which lasts more than one day.

It is best to start your horse on a short competitive trail ride, such as a 10-mile one, before you enter a longer trail ride. On this short ride, the horse will get acquainted with trail terrain and timing, as well as traveling in large groups of horses on the same path. Remember, the trail ride in competition is a new experience for your horse, so you should ready him for it gradually.

If you have no problems with your horse on a 10-mile trail ride, you can begin to condition him for a 40-mile ride. Your training for this ride should begin two or three months before the day of the ride. With the type of conditioning involved, you cannot expect your horse to prepare for such a rugged venture in less than several months' time.

The best way to begin your conditioning for trail competition is to put your horse on a regular riding schedule if he is not on one already. You should be riding your horse daily anyway, but now you will ride him several times each day for a specific amount of time.

If you haven't been riding your horse regularly, your training will take much longer than it will for another rider whose horse is used to daily riding. For the horse who is not used to daily riding, start his trail preparation by riding him once a day for two or three weeks. At first you should ride about 20 minutes a day, gradually working up to almost one hour a day. Once your horse is used to this daily routine, you can begin readying him for a long trail ride.

For a horse who is already in condition and is being ridden daily, you will begin his trail preparation by riding him twice a day. The length of time you ride each time depends on your horse's condition. Some horses will want to go for hours on the first ride of the day, but will be sluggish on the second ride. You should space the riding hours out so that your horse will be willing to go along both times you ride each day.

In the beginning of this conditioning, you may want to start your horse off at only 20 to 30 minutes each time you ride in one day. Ride for the same amount of time on each ride so your horse will become accustomed to regular intervals of riding and resting. This is what you will be doing on the trail ride, so it is best to get your horse used to the routine in advance.

When your horse is used to being ridden twice a day for 30 minutes each time, you can begin to increase your riding time. It should only take your horse a week or two to condition himself to two 30-minute rides per day, since he was already used to being ridden daily. During the third week, you should be riding him twice a day for 45 minutes to an hour in each session.

This conditioning will make your horse stronger day by day, so the length of time you can ride without tiring him should increase rapidly. The more you ride him daily, the stronger he will get.

When you are riding twice a day for one hour at a time, you can step up the riding schedule to riding three times a day for one hour. When on the schedule of three times of riding per day, you should ride in the morning, afternoon, and evening. Soon your horse will be accustomed to being ridden for an hour, resting a few hours, and then being ridden again for an hour. Once he is on this routine, he is on his way to being ready for trail riding competition.

Now that your horse is being ridden three times a day for one hour at a time, you can set the increase in time by yourself. Gradually increase your riding time, keeping it the same each time you ride in one day. Eventually work your horse up to being ridden several hours at a time, three times a day.

When your horse is used to this, take him on an all day trail ride. Pack a lunch and begin in the morning after he has digested his morning feeding. Let him stand for at least one hour after you feed him.

If you have friends who are also preparing for trail riding competition, it would be advantageous to take them along on your all day trail ride. They will provide company for you, as well as getting your horse used to being ridden in a group.

A good schedule for an all day ride is to begin at about 9 in the morning and ride until noon. You may take one or two short breaks during the morning part of the ride, but they

See you later, "pardner," these young riders seem to be saying as they head out toward the trails. The group is following an intelligent and safe pattern by having the children follow the adults. Usually it is best to ride single-file on the trails, but where space permits side-by-side riding, it can provide a bit more companionship. As long as the riders are mounted on good trail horses that do not kick or bite, it is perfectly safe to ride side-by-side at such times. (Photo courtesy the American Quarter Horse Assn.)

should not be longer than 10 or 15 minutes at a time. Stop for a 20 to 30 minute lunch break at noon.

During this break, you should dismount and let your horse rest. Loosen his girth and give him water if some is nearby. Just as you are being allowed to relax for a while, so should your horse. After all, he is doing most of the work.

When you have finished lunch, you may ride until about 2 or 3 in the afternoon. You and your horse should need a break by then, so rest again for 15 or 20 minutes. After that, continue the ride until about 5 p.m. At that time, you and your horse will both be ready for an evening feeding, and should be pretty tired from the long day of riding.

Counting your rest periods, you will have ridden nearly seven hours on this day. This should give your horse a good idea of what to expect on one day of a competitive trail ride, and it should help you develop a sense of timing on the trail.

As you near the date of the actual trail competition, you should take your horse on a long ride every other day. You don't have to keep him out for an all day ride this often, but be sure to ride him 15 to 20 miles every other day. On the in-between days you must still ride your horse, but the rides will be less strenuous. On these days, riding him twice a day for one or two hours at a time will be plenty to keep him in shape.

After you have kept your horse on this schedule of a long ride every other day for two or three weeks, he should be in prime condition for a competitive trail ride. However, do not keep your horse on his rugged riding routine as the days near for the actual competition. Instead, ride him daily, but let him rest. Otherwise, he may be too worn out on the day of the trail ride.

The night before the trail ride, your horse will probably be stabled where the ride is to begin. The ride veterinarian will look your horse over and note any injuries he may already have. This is important, because any injuries your horse sustains while on the trail ride will count against you in the judging.

This foursome takes a pleasant ride on Quarter Horses, which are well-suited to trail and pleasure riding. Trail riding, whether pursued in actual competition or for pleasure, can be an excellent family sport, as these four riders illustrate. (Photo courtesy of the American Quarter Horse Assn.)

If your horse has any such injuries before the ride starts, be sure to point them out to the veterinarian so he will note them on your horse's scorecard.

You should bring your horse's normal feed to the trail ride stables, and feed him the usual amount. You may be feeding him more now that he has been on a rugged training schedule. Any change in amount or type of feed can alter a horse's performance, so be sure to keep these things as constant on the trail ride as they were during the training period.

Give your horse a good grooming the night before the trail ride, and again in the morning before you begin the ride. Good grooming, in addition to properly fitting tack, will help prevent sores which will count against you in the judging. More important, these precautions will help keep your horse free from such discomforts. You want to be fair to your horse at all times, and the judge wants this also.

As a matter of fact, 70 percent of the judging in the trail ride goes to the horse's condition each time the judge checks him. The other 30 percent is determined by time on the trail, so it is easy to see that the condition of the horse is of utmost importance.

One way to keep your horse in good condition on the trail ride is to vary his gaits from time to time. The rider who begins the trail competition at a full gallop will surely wear out his horse too soon, if he is not first disqualified for endangering the other riders. Riders who think that speed is the most important factor on a trail ride are those who lose in the competition. If all you care about is speed, stick to gymkhana games and races. There is no place for a racer on the trail.

Depending on your horse's particular gaits, he may favor one gait that covers ground but does not tire him out. Some western trail horses have a collected lope which is fast enough to cover ground, but slow enough to keep the horse from tiring. The lope can also be very comfortable for the rider, who has to be considered as well.

If your horse is too high spirited to remain collected at the lope for any amount of time, you may do better to jog on the trail ride. A horse with a nice jog can be very comfortable to ride, and many horses can go for miles at the jog without tiring. The jog is a good gait to use often in trail competition, and if you have a horse with a nice jog you are already one step ahead of the game.

The walk should be used occasionally on the trail ride, since it is a means of letting the horse rest without losing too much time. It is also a good transition gait. Use the walk after the trot, and then urge your horse into a lope. After he has loped a while, slow him down to the trot, and then to the walk. Then you can pick up the trot again, and on into a lope. Using the walk in between the other two gaits gives the horse a chance to rest, but keeps him going.

When the horse is walking, do not let him hang his head and plod along. The horse should be kept alert and moving along at all times, except when you stop for a few moments to rest. The rest period is the only time your horse should be allowed to stand still completely. At all other times, you must keep him moving right along.

This changing of gaits and periodic resting is your way of keeping your horse in good condition for the judge, while still keeping track of the clock. This way you are working with an awareness of both elements of judging, while still being fair to your horse and yourself.

There will be times on the trail ride when you will have to slow down to a walk even though you hadn't planned to do so, for example, when the terrain becomes very hilly or rocky. There is no sense in rushing your horse over rocky land, for he may injure his feet or even stumble to his knees. This advice also holds for hilly areas, where your horse could lose his footing if you rush him.

When the terrain becomes extremely rugged, slow your horse down to a walk but still keep him alert. Give him a slack

Heading out on a trail excursion, these riders seem to be having a good time, although they are not following several obvious trail safety rules. Instead of spacing themselves out evenly, they are bunched together, with many riding up on other horses' tails (this is an invitation to be kicked). The riders in front have urged their mounts into a trot, while the riders further back are still at a walk. This can encourage the horses behind to break into a trot, or even to bolt to catch up with the others. (Photo courtesy the American Quarter Horse Assn.)

rein so he can move his head to keep himself in balance, and let him pick his way along slowly. As soon as you have made it through the rough spots, you can resume your horse's normal trail pace.

If by some chance an accident does happen which injures your horse, do not attempt to finish the trail ride as a competitor. Ask another rider to notify the ride veterinarian. Dismount and lead your horse to the nearest place where you can stop and wait for the veterinarian, if your horse can walk. If he is badly injured, just wait where you are until help arrives.

Competition is one thing, but pushing a horse to seriously injure himself is something else altogether. You should be on guard for hazards to your horse at all times, especially on an unfamiliar trail. Objects on the trail path like broken glass, sharp tin cans, and pointed rocks can give your horse a severe cut on the foot. Watch where you are about to ride, and always steer your horse around dangerous objects.

When you reach the finishing point for the day, whether you are on a one day trail ride or one that lasts several days, the judge will look over your horse to see what condition he is in. A scorekeeper will note the time, and will mark down how many minutes early or late you are. Then you will untack your horse, feed him, and bed him down for the night; then you can have a meal yourself.

Most trail rides allow a certain leeway of minutes you may be early or late on arrival at the designated stopping point. However, not many rides will permit you to arrive more than one hour late. If you are that late, you are generally disqualified from the rest of the ride. This is why a competitive trail ride is such a demanding task. The rider must set a certain time in which to finish the ride, while taking into consideration his horse's ability to keep up with this time. Both are important considerations, and it takes good judgment to make both work out evenly on a trail ride.

One factor that can slow your horse down somewhat on the

Trail riding can be a most relaxing sport and hobby, as these two riders well know. A duo in correct western attire, mounted on horses of similar conformation and coloring as these, strike a pleasing picture to onlookers. (Photo courtesy the American Quarter Horse Assn.)

trail is excess weight. An overweight rider can slow his horse down, as can a pack which carries unnecessary items. You want to go to the trail ride prepared, but you shouldn't bring anything which is not absolutely necessary.

The things which you should pack are: food, a rain slicker, a watch, and grooming tools for your horse (such as a hoof pick). These are necessities. Anything else is extra. If it is lightweight and not bulky it may be permissible although it is still something extra, but if it is heavy enough to slow your horse down, the item isn't worth taking.

When you check into the stable for the night, be sure to groom your horse thoroughly. His muscles will need the rubbing to help relax them, and his coat will probably be matted down from the saddle he's been carrying on his back all day. Also, removing dirt from his coat will help protect your horse against the development of saddle sores, which would count against you very much in the judging of the trail ride.

After you have completed the trail ride and the judging is over, you should give your horse some follow-up care. He has been through a rugged few days on the trail, and will need to rest a bit before you put him back on his regular exercise routine.

Groom your horse often, and turn him out in the pasture when he has arrived home from the trail ride. He should be allowed to graze and relax on his first day home.

The next day, you can begin to ride him again, provided he has sustained no injuries or sores from the trail ride. You should keep your horse out for only an hour or so the first day you ride again. Ride him at pleasure gaits, and do not push him to do a lot of hard running. Keep him on easy terrain such as a wide open field with no hills.

After a few days to a week of "easy riding," your horse should be back to normal and ready to continue with his regular routine. If you will be competing regularly in competitive trail rides, keep your horse on his training routine of several hours of riding, two or three times a day.

However, if you intend to keep on with competitive trail rides, be fair to your horse and give him time to recover in between trail competitions. Don't take your horse on a long trail competition every weekend. Rather, space your trail rides out so that you'll be competing no more than two or three times a month. That's only fair to your horse.

Remember that if you wait a month or more between trail competitions, you will have to begin your horse's trail training all over again. If you compete in trail rides with your horse regularly, the rides will keep him in condition for each succeeding ride, as long as you exercise him daily between the rides. If you enter trail rides only every month or two, you'll have to re-train your horse before you enter each competition.

There really isn't much sense in going through the rigorous training for trail competition unless you intend to pursue the sport seriously and constantly. To prepare for just one trail ride is a waste of time since your horse will get out of condition soon after the ride.

Trail riding is not a sport for the rider who wants to compete only occasionally. Although trail riding for pleasure can be done as often or as seldom as you like, competitive trail riding is a demanding sport which requires constant effort and practice.

Just as trail riding for competition requires practice, so does competing in trail classes at horse shows. Fortunately, many of the things you practice for the show ring come in handy on the trail, and vice versa. Showing and trail riding for competition seem to go hand-in-hand. In any case, you're out there to win, and the only way to do that is through constant practice.

8. Fun With Your Trail Horse

By virtue of his versatile nature, the western trail horse can be a lot of fun for his rider. Trail riding and competing in horse show trail classes can be a pleasure, as can entering your trail horse in game events at the same shows.

Most horse shows which offer trail classes also have gymkhana games, and your trail horse should be able to perform well in some of these games. You will have more fun at horse shows if you train your western horse for both trail and game classes, for then you will be able to show all day long, and in a variety of events.

In addition to trail and game classes, you can enter other events in the show. Your practice in gaits and the change of leads will prepare you to enter a western pleasure class. If you ride well, you can also enter western equitation classes. Keeping your horse in good shape will qualify you for a halter showmanship class. This covers just about every class at a horse show for which a stock seat rider is eligible.

Most small horse shows offer these events, usually with about half the classes in the gymkhana games category. This is true for shows of Class "C" or shows which are not classed at all. Gymkhana games are not generally offered in Class "A" and "B" shows.

Gymkhana games are especially popular with spectators and competitors at small shows. The games are exciting because they require fast action on the part of the horses. They are also a lot of fun, because they require that the rider perform tasks which are sometimes hard to do but fun to watch.

Shows which offer gymkhana games are friendly affairs, with the gymkhana riders gathering in groups to watch the attempts of their competitors. Game riders stick close together, since their specialty in riding is so different from that of pleasure or equitation riders. The gymkhana entrants are a good-natured group, and are the first to congratulate a competitor who beats them at the clock in a timed event.

Some of the largest gymkhana events are held out West, where this style of riding is most popular. The games are often mixed in with rodeo events, and provide fun and an exciting time for everyone involved.

Even in the East, gymkhana games are popular. Most horse shows at the large county fairs held in New England each fall offer several gymkhana games.

The games are lively affairs, with horses charging at full speed, stopping on a dime, spinning a turn, and dodging obstacles. Since gymkhana games are run against the clock, many riders take a spill now and then. Usually the gymkhana rider laughs and brushes himself off, while the spectators laugh with him. Occasionally a rider gets seriously hurt in gymkhana events. The sport is done at high speed, with little margin for error. When your horse is at a full gallop and decides not to turn where you have directed him, you can be in for trouble. For this reason, gymkhana games require a lot of practice and an obedient horse, as well as a courageous and thinking rider.

Many of the skills you have taught your trail horse will help make him a good entry for gymkhana events. These games require a great amount of balance and agility in the horse, in addition to mastery of such common skills as the flying change of leads.

Most western trail horses adapt well to gymkhana games. A variety of games cover events for the slow, collected horse and the quick, spirited horse. A trail horse with some spirit will make an excellent gymkhana horse, since he should have enough speed and determination to do well in timed events.

The pure gymkhana horse cannot necessarily adapt to trail events since he may be too high spirited, but the trail horse with a spark of life can compete successfully in gymkhana games. While the gymkhana horse may have a disposition too fiery and unruly for trail events, the western trail horse is tractable but alert by nature. This combination of personality traits makes an excellent prospect for an all-around western performance horse.

The traits needed for a good gymkhana horse are agility, speed, and obedience. The ability to put out a burst of speed, do a quick turn, and stop on a dime is vital for a gymkhana horse who is used in the main game events of barrel racing and pole bending.

Although your trail horse may not be inclined to pour on speed suddenly, he can still make a good game horse. Too many game riders think all they need is a fast, hot horse to win. This is not true, by any means.

A hot horse is sometimes too excitable and headstrong for game competition. Such horses often make their turns too wide, losing precious seconds against the clock. At other times, hot horses will overshoot the obstacle altogether when they start galloping on a straight path.

Your trail horse, since he is obedient enough to stop at your direction and willing enough to move along when you give him the signal, can do better in game events than a pure gymkhana horse.

The best game performance horses are those who are calm

and gentle in pleasure gaits, but who can go into a gallop from a standstill at the starting line. The horse you have to kick and prod will not do well in gymkhana games, and neither will a horse who is uncontrollable at a gallop.

When a horse is at a full gallop in some of these game events, his adrenalin is running high and he has even more strength than usual. A horse with too much spirit may be almost impossible to control when at a full gallop. Obviously, he will not take ribbons in gymkhana classes.

Obedience is the most important thing you can teach your horse for any type of show performance. Your horse should be obedient at the pleasure gaits from your training for trail. To prepare your horse for performance in gymkhana games, you will have to teach him to have this same obedience at a full gallop.

This first step in gymkhana training may take longer than preparing your horse for the specific game events. Once you've taught him to turn and stop from the full gallop, your horse should be able to adapt this and the other skills he has learned to each game.

From practicing for the pleasure part of the trail class, your horse should already know how to halt from the walk, trot, and lope. He should also be able to begin all of these gaits from the standstill. Now you will have to teach him to do the same thing at the gallop.

There is no particular way to teach your horse to obey at a gallop, except to try it first and see what happens. If your horse takes the bit in his teeth and refuses to slow down from the gallop, steer him in a circle until he slows down enough for you to control his direction. This will keep him from bolting with you, and it should show you that you'll first have to teach your horse to obey at the gallop before you can concentrate on specific game training.

Once you can keep your horse from bolting at the gallop, practice making him slow down more and more from this pace. By applying rein pressure and shifting your weight further back and deeper into the saddle, you should be able to slow your horse from the gallop into a collected lope.

Slightly stronger and more steady rein pressure at the gallop should induce your horse to slow down to a trot or jog. If your horse is accustomed to voice commands at each gait, using your voice should help him to respond more quickly to your directions to slow down to whatever gait you desire.

Getting your horse to slow down from a gallop to a walk is not a simple matter. If you apply too light a pressure on the reins, your horse may slow down only to a jog. On the other hand, if your rein pressure is too strong, your horse may come to a sudden halt.

To slow down from the gallop to a walk, you will have to apply firm rein pressure, without tugging on the horse's mouth. When the horse begins to slow down, lessen the pressure. Then, when you feel him slowing almost to a walk, apply slight leg pressure to discourage him from stopping altogether. Giving the horse a gentle squeeze with your legs will urge him to keep moving, while the rein pressure discourages him from moving faster than a walk.

This will take a lot of practice. Slowing from the gallop is easy to practice while you are on your daily pleasure ride, without taking separate time for a training session. This way, your horse doesn't even realize you are training him.

Since you will vary your horse's gaits often on your daily pleasure ride, it won't mean much extra work to use the gallop a bit more often than usual. Practice a transition to and from the gallop from all three gaits at various times on your daily ride. Don't overdo the gallop, or your horse will tire of the transitions. The gallop requires a great amount of physical exertion from your horse, so be careful not to overtire him while practicing your transitions.

Your horse should be quite adept at changing his gaits to and from the gallop after about a month of such practice. Now you can work on getting your horse to halt from the gallop and to start the gallop from a standstill.

The halt from the gallop is a touchy thing to practice. You have to apply enough rein pressure to slow your horse's motion immediately, without hurting his mouth. If you have a calm horse who will not bolt at the gallop, you may want to practice the halt from the gallop using a hackamore bridle so you cannot harm his tender mouth. Even when using a hackamore, you should not apply too much pressure. A hackamore can damage a horse's nose if it is jerked on, so use the hackamore with care, just as you would a bit.

To practice the halt from the gallop, begin by having your horse halt from a collected lope. Then start him at a gallop. After he has traveled some distance at a hard gallop, give him the verbal command "whoa" at the same time as you apply the rein pressure. Push your weight into your stirrups and sit deep and back. This should cause your horse to settle his weight in his hindquarters, which will make him slow down to a halt.

Don't expect your horse to get the hang of this immediately. It is unnatural for the horse to come to such a sudden stop and it will take him some time to learn how. By nature, the horse will go down gradually through the gaits to come to an eventual stop. He will gallop, lope, trot, jog, walk, and then halt. You must teach him to capsulize these steps, skipping the transition steps and stopping immediately from the gallop.

Starting the gallop from a standstill may also be difficult to teach your horse, but it shouldn't take as long as teaching him the halt from the gallop. Frightened horses automatically bolt into a gallop from a standstill, so it will not be too unnatural for your horse to learn the departure at the gallop.

Some horses will require leg pressure, a kick, or even spurs to effect a gallop from a standstill. Such horses are often seen in gymkhana circuits, but you are better off with a horse who will willingly begin a gallop from any gait.

There are several tricks which good gymkhana riders use to urge their mounts to gallop from a standstill at the starting line. Spinning the horse in circles a few times can help him start off at a gallop. As the horse curves out of the circle's arc, his front legs are lifted off the ground and can automatically bound off into a gallop if the rider gives him the proper signal.

Some horses are so spirited they require only a slackening of the reins to get them to begin a gallop from a standstill. Other horses respond better to verbal encouragement. Frequently you will hear riders whooping like Indians in gymkhana events. Their horses respond by breaking into a sudden gallop when they hear the rider make such loud noises.

Once your horse has become accustomed to gymkhana games, he will understand that you want him to start off like a bullet from the starting line. Some gymkhana horses act like lambs outside the game ring, but become devils the minute they set foot inside it. They know that they are supposed to gallop as fast as they can, and their personalities reflect this knowledge.

Every second counts in timed gymkhana events. If your horse starts at a lope and then breaks into a gallop a few steps later you may come in second or third instead of first. That is why it is important to train your horse to go immediately from a standstill to a gallop.

If your horse has trouble doing this, there are ways to get around it in the game ring. Instead of starting right at the start line, run your horse around behind the line. By the time he passes the starting line, he may have worked up enough speed to have started a gallop.

Another thing you can do to get your horse to gallop before he passes the starting line is to lope him behind the line for a few moments. When you are ready to cross the line, pull your horse in a quick turn toward the obstacle you're heading for. This sharp turn will cause the horse to spin a bit and can urge him to begin at a fast lope or a gallop.

Just as it is important to pass the starting line at a gallop, you must also pass the finish line as fast as you can. Do not try to stop right on the finish line. Pass the line at a full gallop instead, and slow down afterward. This may be difficult if you have a headstrong horse, because the finish line is only a few feet from the out gate in some rings.

If your horse has a tendency to either jump the out gate, crash into it, or rush through it if it is open, you'll have to try to turn him around the ring as soon as he passes the finish line. As an extra precaution, ask the gate attendant to keep the gate closed until your horse has slowed down.

Another thing to keep in mind, especially during your training for timed events, is to have your horse make his turns as close to the obstacle as possible. In events like the barrel race and pole bending, which are based on the horse's time through a series of opposite turns, you will make better time if your horse cuts as close to the obstacle as he can. When you are racing against the clock around obstacles, your horse will be making sharp turns at high speeds and he must always be in balance and on the correct lead, or he may fall down.

Another danger in such games is the chance of you striking your inside leg against the obstacle your horse is turning around. Many a barrel racer has had his leg scraped or broken in hitting a barrel, so you'll have to judge just how close your horse can go to the obstacle without injuring you.

Now that you are familiar with the idea of timed events, you can look into each specific event to determine what training is involved and whether your horse is suited to performance in the game.

BARREL RACING

Barrel racing is the most demanding timed event for both horse and rider. The difficulty in mastering barrel racing is seen

Barrel racing requires a great amount of strength, speed, and agility in the horse. It is vital the horse know his proper leads in order to gallop around a barrel at this sharp angle without losing his balance. (Photo courtesy the American Quarter Horse Assn.)

in the fact that it is the highest-paying competitive gymkhana game. Top barrel racers earn $20,000 per year or more—as much as a successful businessman.

Just as the businessman must work for his position, so must the serious barrel racer. This rider and his horse work every day of the year because this is the only way to remain on top. Anyone who wants to excel in barrel racing has a long hard road ahead of him.

For the rider whose profession is barrel racing, one horse is used only for the barrels and for no other riding. However, if you enter barrel racing only as a fun alternative for your trail horse, you may use your all-purpose western performance horse. You may not do well if you compete in a barrel racing show circuit, but you should be able to compete in barrel races at small horse shows with gymkhana events open to all riders.

In order to tackle such a demanding sport, both horse and rider must be in top shape. It is unfair to ask an old horse to compete in constant barrel racing, for the work may be too much for him. More than one horse has died of a heart attack during a barrel race on a hot summer day. Don't ask more of your horse than he is healthy enough to give.

A horse who has not been exercised regularly is in no condition to begin barrel race training. Before you begin his barrel training, put your horse on a regular daily exercise routine. He should be accustomed to being ridden at least two or three hours a day, and should be able to lope some distance without becoming winded, before you start his barrel race training.

Even if your horse is in good physical condition, there is still a certain amount of preparation to be done before you begin his barrel training. Your horse must be readied for the event by practicing the flying change of leads, loping figure eights, and clover leaf patterns at the lope.

The clover leaf is the pattern of the barrel race (see diagram). It is best to lope him in this pattern, with no markers, before you ever take him around the barrels. Let your horse

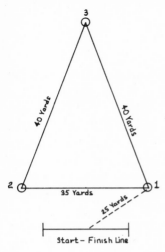

The set-up for the barrel race consists of three barrels, spaced at the designated distances. These barrels are numbered showing the course run "to the right," which is usually preferred at shows. Some shows will allow you to ride the course to either side.

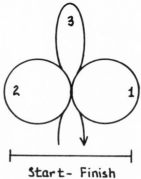

Start- Finish

The "clover leaf" pattern of the barrel race is usually visualized by inexperienced gymkhana riders as actually resembling a three-leaf clover. Although this is the basic pattern of the event, a rider who makes such wide curves around the barrels will lose many valuable seconds in this timed event.

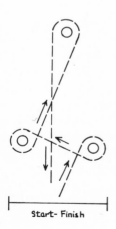

Start- Finish

In more realistic terms, the barrel race pattern, run "to the right," looks like this. When running from one point to another over a good distance, the horse does not move in a curved line, but in a perfectly straight line. Since the shortest distance between two points is a straight line, and since you're going for time here, the straighter the line and the closer the curve around the barrel, the better your time will be in the barrel race.

get the idea of the pattern before you ask him to confront barrels.

The best way to introduce your horse to barrel racing is to acquaint him with your training area. An enclosed ring is best, but if one isn't available there are substitutes. Sometimes a deserted gravel pit is good, if the walls are secure and do not spill loose gravel, but any safe isolated area will be suitable.

Be sure to use the area only for barrel training, so your horse will know that it is time for work the minute he sets foot inside the area. Never use his pasture for training. The horse regards his pasture as his personal home, to relax and act in as he pleases. Your horse deserves this dignity, so keep his pasture and your training area separate.

In choosing a training area, remember that the fewer distractions, the better. You want your horse to concentrate on the lesson you are giving him, and you can't expect him to give you his undivided attention if he can see his stablemates frolicking in the pasture.

In performing timed events in the show ring, your horse will have to cope with distractions and learn to ignore them. That will come later and he will gradually get used to the common noises at horse shows. But during his training, your horse has enough to handle without worrying about distractions.

An indoor ring offers the least distractions, but few horsemen are lucky enough to have one available. On the other hand, you may be better off training outdoors if you expect to do most of your competing outdoors. A barrel horse who is used to the protected indoor ring may become nervous and forget much of his training when you switch him to an outdoor show ring.

The best training area is the ring where you expect to do most of your showing, if it is possible for you to ride there. Many local stables have barrels already set up in one ring, and let neighboring competitors practice in the ring.

This will acquaint your horse with not only the ring and the show grounds, but also with the barrels you'll be riding in shows. Barrels are often painted in different colors, and a new pattern can alarm a novice barrel horse.

If you train your horse at home with solid-colored barrels, he may spook in the show ring when he is confronted with striped barrels. It is best to avoid this in the first place by acquainting your horse with the show barrels.

This is the general rule in all types of horse training, especially in timed events. Any new obstacle, or even a familiar one painted a different way, can be enough to send a newly trained horse into a frenzy.

To prevent your horse from spooking his first time around the barrels, lead him up to the obstacles slowly and confidently. Let him sniff the barrels and push them with his nose if he wishes. Nothing is worse than a horse who spooks halfway around a barrel, so it is best to prevent this by letting the horse "meet" the barrels while standing still.

Your first trip through the clover-leaf pattern around the barrels will be done at a walk. This serves to introduce the pattern and the barrels to the horse. On your first day of training at the barrels do not proceed any faster than a walk through the pattern.

If your horse goes through the pattern confidently, you can trot him through the barrels on the second day. When he can travel through the pattern at a fast trot, you are ready to begin serious barrel training at the lope.

At this point, you must begin to make speed a consideration. The fastest way between two points is a straight line, and you must incorporate this fact into your barrel running. Although your early barrel training will not center on the time clock, it is wise to lope your horse in a pattern that will mean fewer seconds later when you try it at a gallop.

You should get your horse into the habit of going through the barrels by the shortest possible route. Do this from the start of your training. If you allow the horse to take wide turns around the barrels now, he will tend to do the same later on when you are running against the clock. You'll only be creating problems for yourself if you allow the horse to go through the barrels any way he chooses.

As you go from one barrel to another, your horse should be running in a straight line. When he nears the barrel he will have to edge out a little to begin his turn, but he should not start to run in a circular pattern until just before he reaches the barrel. A horse who takes wide, arcing turns around the barrels will never be a winner. Since the name of the game is speed, the quickest way to get through the course is to run a straight line between the barrels and make a sharp turn around each one. You want your horse to stick as close as possible to the barrel when he turns around it, without striking the barrel. Watch out for your legs and feet, or your leg can be severely scraped by a horse who cuts too close to the barrels.

Every time you practice at the barrels, no matter at what gait, ride as though you were racing against the clock. Make your horse take sharp turns at the barrels, and reward him when he does well. A pat on the neck and a "good boy" will do for praise.

When you first start your horse's serious practice at the barrels, you may find it easier to use two hands on the reins. Some barrel trainers even prefer to begin a horse at the task with an English bridle, since a snaffle bit will not hurt his mouth.

It takes quite a bit of strength and pressure to pull a horse around the barrels the first few times until he gets the idea. If you use a snaffle bit, your horse probably will not fight the pressure. Using a bit which is too severe may make the horse dislike barrels because he will feel as though he is being punished every time you pull him around in the turns.

Reining with two hands may be very helpful, or even completely necessary, when you are training a new horse for the barrels. If you neck rein a horse around a turn, he may tend to fight the pressure and refuse to turn sharply enough. On the

The importance of staying at the same pace as your mount in
barrel racing is illustrated here, with this horse and rider very
much out of timing with each other. The horse is dashing toward
the barrel at an angle which shows he may nearly topple over
in another stride or so. The rider is totally out of balance, with
her arm waving wildly in the air and her foot out of the stirrup.
Her weight has slipped back, fighting the motion of the horse. Instead, she should be leaning with the animal in towards the turn.
(Photo courtesy the American Quarter Horse Assn.)

other hand, if you pull the horse's head around with one rein, he has no choice. This way, you can be the one to determine how sharply your horse should turn around the barrels. If you pull only lightly, he will make a wide turn; if you pull his head way around, he will make a turn very close to the barrel.

Obviously, your horse may not appreciate you pulling him around this way. He may respond by doing exactly what you want, in order to get you to stop pulling so hard. Or he may come to dislike the whole process if you push the training too hard.

There are two ways to rein a horse through a turn by the two-handed English method. If your horse does not respond well to one, try the other.

The proper way to turn an English horse is to draw one hand back toward the opposite hip bone. If you are turning to the right, your right hand would pull the right rein diagonally toward your left hip bone. Your hands remain over the horse's withers.

This method pulls the horse's head around in a very effective way. When you pull like this, the horse must follow in the direction his head is turning in order to keep the rest of his body in balance throughout the motion. The action is a smooth one, and is always done in the show ring by English riders.

The other method of reining English through a turn is called using the "leading rein." This method entails exactly what it says—you use the rein to lead the horse around into the turn. To do this, your hand reaches out to the side, about a foot away from the horse's withers. You must shorten your turning rein to effect this turn, and will be holding it closer to the bit.

The leading rein is used in turning green horses who have not yet been schooled to respond to the proper way of English reining through a turn. You may have to use this on your horse when he is learning the barrels, for it gives him a direct pull to turn the way you want.

However, if your horse is well schooled in western neck reining, he may perform the barrels just as well for you this way. You might need to help your horse a little at first by pushing on the side of his neck. If you are turning right around the barrel, you would lay the reins over his neck with your hand to the right side, while you push gently on the left side of his neck.

This is one way to make the transition in your horse's training from English reining in barrel turns to proper western neck reining. After he has responded well to English reining, you will want your horse to do the same when you neck rein him. Pushing lightly on his neck will encourage your horse to follow through the turns in the same manner he did when you used two hands on the reins.

A really well-trained western horse will even respond to your pushing on his neck alone, without using the reins. When you lay your hand on the side of such a horse's neck, he will automatically turn in the opposite direction. Obviously, a horse like that would be quite easy to train for an event like barrel racing.

So, depending on your horse's training and capabilities, your job of training may be easier or harder. Once you have gotten him to take turns close to the barrels at a lope, you are ready to begin his training at the gallop.

The fastest way to run the barrels is to get a running start over the starting line, and head at full speed straight toward the first barrel, slightly toward the inside of the barrels. As you approach the barrel, your horse will have to slow down a bit.

The best barrel horses barely slow before the turn. Like a race car driver, these horses slow down slightly before the turn, and then proceed through it at full speed. However, there is no way a horse can gallop as fast in a circle as he can in a straight line.

Still, top barrel horses seem to whirl right through the clover leaf pattern. For top speed, they nose right into the barrels.

Fine balance is required of both horse and rider at this speed around a circle. As he makes the turn, the horse's body will be at a very sharp angle to the barrel. The best barrel horses turn so sharply that the rider can touch the ground with his outside leg. If you can do this, you will know your horse is really performing well.

You will make your fastest time through the barrels if your horse gets a running start and pours on a burst of speed as he comes around each barrel turn, heading toward the next one. Encourage your horse to do so by letting your hand go forward with the reins, and urging him on with your body position.

When your horse has turned the three barrels and is on his way "home" (to the finish line), open him up completely. Give him a slack rein and ask him to give you as much speed as he can. Cross the finish line at full speed.

If your horse is really running fast, or if the out gate is too close to the finish line, you may need to ride your horse around the rail of the ring for a short distance to slow him down. Don't go rushing through the out gate at full clip, or you may injure a spectator or spook someone's horse.

After your horse has run the barrels, dismount, loosen his cinch, and let him rest. If it is a hot day, walk him around a bit and then let him have a few sips of water after he has cooled off.

The event is a strenuous one for your horse, so it is only fair to let him rest. Don't enter him in the very next gymkhana game, unless it is a much less strenuous one. It is unfair to tire a horse out by entering him in every class at a show. He cannot perform at his best when he is exhausted.

POLE BENDING

Next to barrel racing, pole bending is the most popular gymkhana event. This event takes just about as much strength and stamina as the barrel race, and requires the same amount of training for your horse.

Unlike the barrel race—which depends on the horse's speed at three open turns—pole bending requires the horse to make a series of quick turns. Several poles are set in a row. The horse runs straight to one side of them, weaves in and out through the poles to one end, turns and weaves back through them again to the other end, and then races straight for the finish line (see illustration).

This race depends on the horse's ability to make a quick change of leads; otherwise he will trip himself. It is up to your horse to take care of this matter, since the action is too fast for you to signal the change of leads to him. Most horses do it naturally anyway, just to keep in balance.

Obviously, an agile horse will do best in the pole bending race. Your horse should be athletic, surefooted, and able to make fast and sharp turns.

In pole bending, your horse will not be at such a sharp angle to the ground as he is in barrel racing, for he will be making the turns closer to the obstacle. To spectators, it will look like your horse is running a straight line through the poles, but he is actually skipping side-to-side past each pole as he goes by. The horse's body remains fairly upright, leaning slightly toward the pole he is turning around. If he leans too much, his body or your foot may knock the pole down.

The standard rules call for the event to be comprised of six poles spaced 21 feet apart. Small local horse shows may not abide by the official rules, but all classed shows will.

When you practice pole bending at home, it is advisable to place the poles at the required distance apart. This way your horse can learn how to gauge his turns exactly to get through the poles in the quickest way, and you will become accustomed to the degree of turning necessary for your horse.

This spacing is more important in pole bending than it is in barrel racing, for the degree of turning around a barrel is always the same. The barrels are spaced much more widely apart than the poles. If your horse is trained on poles that are 25 feet

Pole bending is a demanding event in gymkhana which requires a good deal of practice—that means every day, not just before a show. This horse and rider team obviously have much practice behind them, for they seem to be moving together in a mutual effort at the task. (Photo courtesy the American Quarter Horse Assn.)

apart, he may not be able to turn quickly enough in the ring when the poles are the regulation 21 feet apart.

If you are going to teach your horse something, it is best to teach him the right way in the first place, but start slowly at the poles, gradually working up to a gallop through them.

First, let him look the poles over and sniff them. Once his curiosity is satisfied, ask him to walk through the poles. Start at one end and go through the pattern just as you would in the ring. Be sure to let your horse rest periodically when training for the poles, or he may become dizzy from all the turning.

Just as you may have done when training for barrel racing, you might want to rein your horse by one of the English methods when you start him at the poles. It depends on how well your horse turns and how long it takes him to get the idea of the pole bending pattern.

If you do rein English here, you will probably need to use the method of the leading rein. Since the turns are so quick and sharp in pole bending, the proper method of English reining through a turn may not work well for you.

There is also the chance that your horse may respond perfectly well to western neck reining at the poles. He may be quite used to the idea of a series of sharp turns if you have already trained him for the barrels.

Whichever way you rein him through the turns, don't push the training too hard all at once. At first, ride him through the poles for about ten minutes a day. You can increase his training time later.

In an event like this, it is best to train for very short periods with breaks in between. Horses easily tire of weaving through poles. To avoid turning your horse sour toward pole bending, give him plenty of rest and another diversion in between training periods.

In all phases of his training, it is important to reward your horse whenever he responds correctly. Verbal praise will suffice. Don't make a habit of giving your horse a food treat every

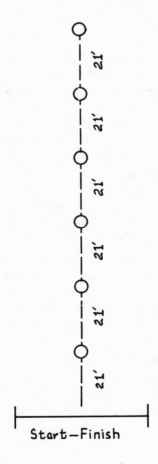

The basic diagram for the pole bending race shows six poles, evenly spaced out with 21-feet in between each (including the distance from the starting line to the first pole).

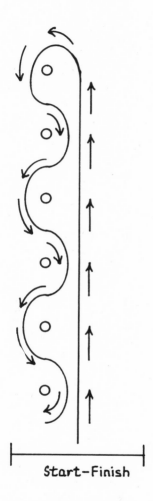

Start-Finish

To run the poles "to the left," the rider runs a straight line from the starting point to the end of the six poles. He weaves in and out around each pole until he is back near the starting point. This completes the first half of the course.

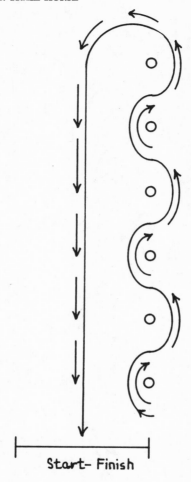

Start- Finish

To complete the event, the rider continues on course, this time running around the other side of the poles, in the same motion of weaving in and out. Since he began this pattern by running a straight line along the right side of the line of poles, he will finish it by riding a curve around the left of the last barrel, and running a straight line towards the finish point, along the left side of the line of poles. To run the course "to the right," the process is exactly the same, only in reverse directions.

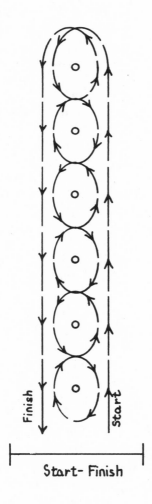

The pole bending race, showing the entire course, as run "to the left."

time he responds well, or he will continue to expect a treat even after he has completed his training at the event.

After you have walked your horse through the poles a few times, you can trot him through the next day. Even at the trot, make him stick close to the poles. Wide turns here will count against you on the time clock.

The third day, you may lope your horse through the series of poles. You may find it a bit difficult to keep him on course at first, but developing control here is vital. Later you will be riding a galloping horse through the obstacle, which will require even more control on your part.

Occasionally your horse may miss a turn and run right past a pole. This can be due to his obstinacy, or to your failure to steer him through the course correctly. If he does make this mistake, do not scold or beat him. Just go back to the beginning of the poles and try it again until he does it properly.

When your horse is loping through the poles well and making close turns, you can start racing against the clock in your training. Riding through the poles at a gallop can be rather difficult, and this part of the training may take even longer than the early stages.

Since you must first race down to the far end of the poles before you begin weaving back through them, many horses have the tendency to run right past the last pole. At a full gallop, a spirited horse may become too excited to suddenly slow down and start turning around poles.

If you do not have very strong arms, you may have a hard time bringing your horse around to the poles. A galloping horse can be almost impossible to stop unless he has been trained to obey the rider at all gaits.

Your horse should already have learned to do this before you begin his training at any obstacles; otherwise you will be wasting your money on class entry fees, as your horse will not make good time if he overshoots the poles.

As you near the last pole, start to lean slightly toward it.

Your shift in balance will tell the horse you are preparing to have him turn in that direction. As you do this, begin to rein your horse into the turn. If your horse is well schooled enough at the poles, he should not run past them. He should understand what he is expected to do at the obstacle, and should perform that way every time.

In order to do well in competition at any timed event, your horse must be tractable. Until you can control him completely at the gallop, you have no business in the show ring for gymkhana games.

FLAG RACE

The flag race is similar to pole bending. This event involves running from two buckets at opposite ends of the ring and switching the flags which are stuck in them (see illustration).

The race can be run in slight variations, starting with or without a flag in the rider's hand. Basically, the flag race requires the rider to gallop his horse to one bucket, stop long enough to take out the flag and replace it with another flag already in his hand, and then rush to the second bucket and do the same thing.

This is similar to pole bending in that the horse runs a fairly straight line, and is required to slow down at the end of the ring after pouring on a full burst of speed.

It may be difficult to get your horse close enough to the bucket because he may be afraid of the flag in it. Wind will make the flag wave, which may make the horse nervous. However, once your horse is accustomed to the event, he should have no qualms about the flag.

To win at this event, you need a fast horse who can stop suddenly and then pour on speed again. To save time, some winning riders do not bring their horses to a complete stop at the bucket. Instead, they slow the horse down enough to make a quick exchange of the flags. If you can do this, all the better.

The flag race does not require a great amount of practice.

As long as your horse will slow down from a gallop and near the bucket, you have it made.

This can be a fun event for both riders and spectators. It is an exciting race, made colorful by the fluttering flag carried in the air by the rider. Since much of the event has the horse running at full speed, it carries all the excitement of a horse race. The spectators will urge you on, yelling western phrases to excite your horse to run faster. All in all, the flag race can be very enjoyable.

BROOM POLO

Broom polo is not always a standard event at gymkhana shows, but is a fun event that many smaller shows offer. It requires little training, so it is something almost anyone can enter.

In this event, the rider is handed a broom which he will use to push a ball the length of the show ring. Sometimes this is done in teams, but it can be dangerous with too many riders unless the ring is large enough.

Broom polo is also fun for spectators. The efforts of the rider to move the ball along with a broom from atop his horse can make very funny antics. As long as your horse does not shy from the broom or the ball, he will do well at broom polo.

TABLETOP CAPER

Like broom polo, this is not a standard event at all shows, but it is a favorite with many riders. The event involves the rider rushing on horseback to a table which is in the middle of the ring. When he nears the table, the rider dismounts and leads his horse toward it.

The fun begins when the rider climbs onto the table and tries to mount his horse from there. Some horses refuse to get close enough to the table and the rider has to take a flying leap onto the horse's back.

In most shows, the rider has the option of competing in this event with or without a saddle on his horse. Some riders find it quicker to dismount and mount again without bothering with a saddle and stirrups. Others find that they slide right over the horse's back and onto the ground when they try to mount an unsaddled horse from the table top.

Of course, this can be very amusing for spectators, and the riders enjoy themselves as well. Often a horse will line right up beside the table and then suddenly move away when the rider jumps toward his back. Many riders in this class take a spill, but it is all in good humor.

There is little you can do to prepare your horse for competition in the tabletop caper except to practice it at home. If you can get your horse to sidepass up to the table and line himself up parallel to it, you will make better time.

Many riders make the mistake of jumping onto the table and tugging at the reins to get their horse over to it. Usually this will result in the horse walking straight toward the table, making it difficult for the rider to mount again.

Once you have mounted from the table, you will urge your horse to gallop to the finish line. If you have a hard time mounting and take more than one minute, the judge will probably disqualify you and ask you to leave the ring so you won't waste time.

FANNY RIDE

Unlike the other gymkhana games already mentioned, the fanny ride is done with all the entrants in the ring together. It is considered a gymkhana game, but it is not a timed event.

The fanny ride is done with all horses bareback. A 12-inch slip of paper is placed 6 inches under the rider's buttocks, with the other half of the paper showing.

At the command of the ring announcer, the riders urge their horses into the various gaits. A rider is disqualified if he loses his slip of paper or if he does not respond immediately to the directions of the announcer.

The fanny ride is a test of the rider's ability to stick to the horse's back at all gaits. The trot will eliminate many riders right off the bat, except those who can grip well with their legs or who have a horse with a smooth jog-trot.

It is relatively easy to keep the paper under you while the horse walks and lopes, for these are smooth gaits. Remember to sit back, or you will lose the slip of paper.

Many riders are eliminated when the announcer asks for a change of gaits, especially from the lope to a halt. You really have to be a good bareback rider and have a smooth-gaited horse to do well in this event.

The fanny ride is a lot of fun, especially when the competition has been narrowed down to the last two riders who still have their strips of paper. At that point, the ring announcer will ask for rapid and sudden changes of gait and direction to determine who will take first place in the class.

Since all the contestants are in the ring together, the fanny ride creates a great degree of competition, but most riders will be laughing and enjoying the event.

BREAK AND OUT

Another gymkhana game which is done with all riders in the ring is the break and out contest. Like the fanny ride, this game uses a slip of paper and is not run against the clock.

Two riders compete as a team in this event. They hold a strip of paper between them, and ride side by side. At the command of the ring announcer, they put their horses into the various gaits.

As the name indicates, any team which breaks its slip of paper is out of the contest. If a rider drops his side of the paper, the team is also disqualified.

To win at this event, the two horses should be of about the same size and speed. The more closely their gaits coincide, the easier it will be for the riders to stay together without tearing the paper.

Sometimes teams enter on what look like twin horses: the two mounts are of the same size and coloring, and have the same way of going in every gait. If the riders dress alike, one will look like a mirror-image of the other. The spectators enjoy watching teams like this, and will often root for them to win.

OTHER GAMES

In addition to these common gymkhana events, each show may offer some other new games. Anyone can invent a timed event or a class gymkhana game by using his imagination and his sense of fun.

If a game that you have never heard of is listed in the program, ask a show official what it involves. You should always know what you are up against before you enter the ring.

One thing that especially makes gymkhana games fun is that they are not subject to the whims of the judge. A timed event is won cut-and-dry by whoever makes the best time. In a class game like the fanny ride, the last rider who still has his paper is declared the winner.

This means that when you win one of these events, you have done it fair and square. You don't have to worry about influencing the judge. All you have to contend with is the time clock and your own riding ability.

Only one thing will count against you in gymkhana events: cruelty to the horse. Since timed events are exciting, some riders try to get the best time by spurring or beating their horses. Any good show will state in its program that behavior like this means immediate disqualification.

You will also be disqualified if you do not follow the game rules exactly. Gymkhana riders are an honest bunch, and they frown upon anyone who tries to cheat in a game to win. If you do this, you may be barred from competing in any other class during the rest of the show.

Gymkhana riding is fun, and you should be a good sport at all times. The good sportsmanship displayed by the majority of game riders is what makes the events so much fun. Everyone is there for a good time and some clean competition.

The spirit of friendship abounds at gymkhana shows. Even riders who constantly compete in games against each other are often the best of friends. If one beats the other at a timed event, the rider who lost will be among the first to congratulate the winner. This is a refreshing change from the daily life many people lead. It is an attempt to return to the old days of the West, when "fun" meant testing your horse out against your neighbor's.

It has been said that "simple pleasures are the best," and competition in gymkhana games bears this out. For a serious trail rider, entering these games can be a pleasant change of pace. At any rate, it is pure fun. Enjoy it.

Afterword

The western trail horse is one of the most versatile horses you will ever meet, and this makes him a lot of fun. How many ribbons he wins depends on how much time you invest in his training—the western trail horse is what you make him.

A horse like this is a pleasure to own, and can bring you much pride with his show ring performance. He can compete in pleasure, trail, jumping, and gymkhana classes, and can also do well on competitive trail rides.

Since your horse is so versatile, you can enter him in as many horse show events as you wish. You may want to specialize in one type of event if your horse has a particular talent in any given area of competition.

In any event, your western trail horse will do his best for you. Be proud of him, and take care of him well. Your horse is a faithful friend, and he deserves the very best you can give him. Care for him and respect him, and your horse will be a pleasure for years to come.

Index